The **NO-NONSENSE GUIDE** to

THE ARMS TRADE

T0126180

'Publishers have created lists of short books that discuss the questions that your average [electoral] candidate will only ever touch if armed with a slogan and a soundbite. Together [such books] hint at a resurgence of the grand educational tradition... Closest to the hot headline issues are *The No-Nonsense Guides*. These target those topics that a large army of voters care about, but that politicos evade. Arguments, figures and documents combine to prove that good journalism is far too important to be left to (most) journalists.'

Boyd Tonkin,
The Independent,
London

About the author
Nicholas Gilby led Campaign Against Arms Trade (CAAT)'s efforts to expose the corruption in British arms deals with Saudi Arabia. In 2008, he defeated Britain's Foreign and Commonwealth Office in an Information Tribunal to force the disclosure of many documents concerning corruption in Britain's arms deals with Saudi Arabia.

As a former member of CAAT's Steering Committee, he was closely involved in CAAT's attempt to force the Serious Fraud Office to re-open its corruption investigation relating to BAE's arms deals with Saudi Arabia, as well as CAAT's efforts to combat the espionage carried out against it.

His research on arms trade corruption has been featured in *The Guardian* (and on the newspaper's 'BAE files' website), TV (BBC Newsnight and Al Jazeera) and in an academic journal. He was previously a director of TAPOL, the Indonesia Human Rights Campaign.

About the New Internationalist
The **New Internationalist** is an independent not-for-profit publishing co-operative. Our mission is to report on issues of global justice. We publish informative current affairs and popular reference titles, complemented by world food, photography and gift books as well as calendars, diaries, maps and posters – all with a global justice world view.
    If you like this *No-Nonsense Guide* you'll also enjoy the **New Internationalist** magazine. Each month it takes a different subject such as *Trade Justice*, *Afghanistan* or *Clean Start: building a fairer global economy*, exploring and explaining the issues in a concise way; the magazine is full of photos, charts and graphs as well as music, film and book reviews, country profiles, interviews and news.

To find out more about the **New Internationalist**, visit our website at **www.newint.org**

The **NO-NONSENSE GUIDE** to

THE ARMS TRADE

Nicholas Gilby

The No-Nonsense Guide to The Arms Trade

First published in the UK by
New Internationalist™ Publications Ltd
Oxford OX4 1BW, UK
www.newint.org
New Internationalist is a registered trade mark.

First printed 2002.
This new edition published in 2009.

Cover image: Qilai Shen/Panos

Series editors: Troth Wells and Chris Brazier
Design by New Internationalist

 Printed on recycled paper by TJ Press International, Cornwall, UK,
who hold environmental accreditation ISO 14001.

British Library Cataloguing-in-Publication Data.
A catalogue record for this book is available from the British Library.

Library of Congress Cataloguing-in-Publication Data.
A catalogue record for this book is available from the Library of Congress.

ISBN 978-1-906523-17-6

Foreword

As the world faces 'new' crises over the climate and the global economy, some people might be tempted to ignore 'old' issues like the global arms trade. We do so at our peril. As Nicholas Gilby writes in this excellent, succinct study, arms profiteers are looking to make money from new forms of potential conflict, which will be exacerbated unless the arms trade is halted.

The world's five largest arms exporters – the US, Russia, Germany, France and Britain – together sold around $20 billion worth of weapons in 2007. The recipients include an array of human rights abusers, countries in conflict and poor, sometimes fragile states whose élites are wasting their countries' scarce resources. These weapons have sometimes helped put down popular demonstrations against repressive regimes or exacerbated internal conflicts and human rights abuses, as in the Darfur region of Sudan or in Colombia. Arms exports can also raise tensions between rivals and increase the prospect of regional wars, as with the arming of India and Pakistan or China and Taiwan. Indeed, some arms exporters, notably the US and Britain, have a habit of arming both sides in regional disputes. US weapons are present in half the world's armed conflicts.

The biggest arms pushers are, with the exception of Russia, all member states of NATO; they are Western states that regularly preach about how the rest of the world is endangering us. The reality is that it is 'we' who often pose the biggest threats to world peace. Nowhere is this clearer than in the case of Britain, which sold £45 billion ($66 billion) worth of arms around the world in New Labour's first decade in power after 1997. Over £100 million of military equipment went to Israel throughout a period of offensive operations in the occupied territories and war with Lebanon. Half a billion pounds worth of British military and related equipment has gone to China, which is supposed to be under an EU arms embargo. Despite British prime ministers posing as the champions of the world's poor, they also continue to sell unaffordable weapons to many African countries.

But as Nicholas Gilby points out, it is not only actual weapons transfers that give cause for concern, but the associated practises of official military training programs, private mercenary companies playing key roles in conflicts, the marketing of arms through international trade fairs, the extent of taxpayer subsidies for military production, and widespread corruption – not to mention espionage by some arms companies against campaigners.

The task of addressing this array of issues is not small and the arms industry is deeply entrenched in many countries. Yet there are some international mechanisms in place that, if deepened and widened, can begin to control the global arms trade. Moreover, in some countries recently, campaigning groups have exposed corruption in arms deals and continue to reveal the costs of arms transfers for human rights and development. Policy-makers are under pressure and the bar is being raised; it is up to us to continue to strive for an end to this business of death, and this study provides an indispensable information tool to help us do so.

Mark Curtis, writer and campaigner
www.markcurtis.info

CONTENTS

Introduction

THE ARMS BUSINESS in today's world tries to maintain a friendly, respectable face, but it is as murky, secretive and amoral as it has always been. So when I was offered the chance to build on the excellent work done by Gideon Burrows when he wrote the first edition of this book, I was pleased to accept.

This updated edition of the *No-Nonsense Guide to The Arms Trade*, like the previous one, attempts to give some background, and provide campaigners and others with material for more questions to arms companies, governments and the military industrial complex the world over. It aims to be a useful tool for spreading information and for future campaigning.

The world is much smaller today, thanks to globalization, with arms companies becoming bigger even than some countries. The response of campaigners has to be similar, if we are to keep up the pressure, linking up with other movements, campaigners and individuals pressing non-violently for peace, justice and a fairer world.

To anyone who asks, 'what is the point?', I have only one reply. We must keep pushing the issues because if we do not, who knows what could happen next? Who knows how many more Tiananmen Squares, East Timors, or Congos would have taken place had not campaigners agitated for arms sales to be restricted, and for action to bring a more just and stable world?

To borrow, but turn around, the weak old challenge of the arms business – 'if we don't sell arms, someone else will' – if we do not keep up the questioning, challenging, direct action, protesting and political lobbying, are we sure someone else would?

I tried to keep changes to the first edition to a minimum, but inevitably quite a lot has changed. Some material needed to be updated, new issues included, and words cut for reasons of brevity.

Occasionally, I did not share Gideon's opinion or perspective. However, as will be apparent to anyone comparing the two editions, I am greatly indebted to the work he did six years ago.

As will be clear from the text and references, I have drawn on a wide range of material from many organizations in what is, inevitably, a brief summary of many issues. The scope and quality of the reports, articles and books available to someone wishing to research a wide variety of arms trade issues is testament to the excellent work of many organizations and individuals. I would like to express my heartfelt thanks to them for making this task much easier than it could have been.

In particular I would like to thank Helen Close and Ian Prichard for their thoughts on the structure when I started work, and to Helen for her comments on the draft manuscript. Albert Beale kindly agreed to check the list of NGO groups at the end of the book. Thanks also to Troth Wells for being a supportive commissioning editor, and to Chris Brazier for his thoughtful editing. Any omissions, errors, or other faults with the book are, of course, entirely my responsibility.

Nicholas Gilby
London, March 2009

1 War in the 21st century

A picture of the changing security environment... The nature of war today... Trends which will affect the level and nature of future conflict... The relevance of the traditional military-industrial complex.

THE ARMS TRADE is no ordinary business. Inextricably linked to the production of weapons, it will therefore have a major influence on war and international relations in this century, directly impacting the lives of many millions of people around the world.

The former senior British and NATO General Sir Rupert Smith has written in his book *The Utility of Force* 'conflict has been, is, and probably always will be an integral element of human society'.[1] As Oxfam has said, 'arms transfers alone do not *cause* armed conflict. Extensive research, however, shows how the availability of, and access to, conventional arms and ammunition can aggravate, intensify, and prolong armed violence'.[2] This is why the arms trade is a serious problem.

This chapter looks at the world the arms companies and dealers operate in. How has the security environment changed since the Second World War and Cold War? What does this mean for the arms industry? What are the trends that will affect levels of conflict and violence in the world in the future?

The changing security environment
The 20th century was the most violent one in human history. Not only did it witness two world wars, and 45 years of major arms-fueled tension between the world's superpowers, it also featured hundreds of localized conflicts, armed border disputes, civil wars, military coups and counter-coups, revolutionary struggles and armed invasions.

Nevertheless, the nature of conflict has changed radically over the last 70 years. Smith has argued that the Second World War marked the culmination of the concept of 'industrial war', a test of each belligerent's military industrial complex, state organization and popular will. The advent of nuclear weapons meant such a conflict could never happen again, for, had a war broken out, within weeks it would have escalated to a nuclear confrontation, resulting in a global holocaust. The vast military machines and industries of each side would have served little purpose. The collapse of Communism across eastern Europe in 1989-91 means the prospect of another major 'industrial war' is now greatly reduced.

Wars between states have still occurred since the Second World War, but they have been in decline. As Smith writes, 'war no longer exists. Confrontation, conflict and combat undoubtedly exist all around the world... [but] war as battle in a field between men and machinery, war as a massive deciding event in a dispute in international relations: such war no longer exists'. Over the last 10 years, only four wars between countries have been fought: Eritrea/Ethiopia (1998-2000), India/Pakistan (in Kashmir, 1997-2003), Iraq/US and allies (2003), and Russia/Georgia (2008).[3] Indeed, the one international war since 2004 only lasted six days. And wars between countries have become less lethal. In 1950 the average such war killed 38,000 people, but in 2006 killed just over 500.[4]

If we look at wars within countries too and define war as a conflict with more than 1,000 battle-related deaths, then the number of wars reported in 2007 (Iraq, Afghanistan, Sri Lanka and Somalia) was the lowest since 1957.[5]

War today

War today is primarily fought within states, either as conflicts over territory or groups fighting against their own government. Indeed, World Bank economist Paul Collier notes, 'civil wars are around ten times as common as international wars'.[6]

These sorts of war do not involve the scale of killing that characterized major 20th-century wars. Between 1946 and 2006, the average war between countries killed 34,677 people per year, while the average internal conflict killed 2,430 people per year.[7]

The Stockholm International Peace Research Institute (SIPRI)[8] records that, over the period 1997-2006, two-thirds of the major armed conflicts that were not international disputes were conflicts over governmental power, with the remainder conflicts over territory. Some of these conflicts are 'internationalized' in that they include troops from a country external to the basic conflict aiding one of the belligerents. Examples today include the NATO intervention in the conflict between the Afghan Government and the Taliban, and the US/British intervention in the conflict between the Iraqi Government and the insurgency.

War today cannot therefore be understood in the traditional sense. It is a confusing picture. As SIPRI has pointed out, there is a 'diversity of armed violence and the erosion of the boundaries between, for example, insurgency, terrorism, sectarian violence and one-sided violence against civilians... in 2007 there was a clear trend towards the further fragmentation of violence in the locations of some of the world's deadliest armed conflicts... this has been accompanied by the diversification of armed groups and the further erosion of the boundaries between different forms of violence'.[9]

Governments increasingly fight groups relying on paramilitary violence or violence from militias. Weak governments in many conflict regions of the world mean the state has often lost its monopoly on violence. Increasingly governments rely on state-backed militias

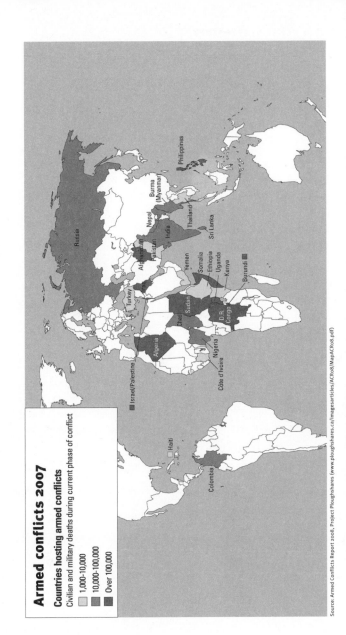

Armed conflicts 2007

Countries hosting armed conflicts
Civilian and military deaths during current phase of conflict

- 1,000–10,000
- 10,000–100,000
- Over 100,000

Source: Armed Conflicts Report 2008, Project Ploughshares (www.ploughshares.ca/imagesarticles/ACR08/MapACR08.pdf)

13

or private contractors to fight their wars.[10] In addition, conflicts less frequently end in 'victory' for one side; since the 1990s there has been an increase in the number of negotiated settlements to conflicts.[11]

According to the Armed Conflicts Report 2008, there were 30 armed conflicts in progress in 26 different countries in 2007. For the first 20 years after 1945, the number of armed conflicts in the world averaged around 20 per year. This rose steadily so that, by the late 1970s, it was at the same level as today. Despite the numbers of armed conflicts having fallen since their post-war peak around 1990, the trend of decline since then appears to have stopped.[12]

Prospects for the future

So what of the future? What are the main threats to peace in the world this century?

There are three primary threats, closely linked.[13]

The first is climate change.[14] Compared to pre-industrial times, the world is getting warmer, and almost all scientists agree this is due to human activities. The warming is caused by the increasing amounts of so-called greenhouse gases (chiefly carbon dioxide) in the atmosphere. Warming causes significant changes to the environment, but on balance most of these are negative.

These create potentially very significant security problems. For example, the 0.75°C of warming that has occurred so far has resulted in 10 to 25 million people being displaced in Africa due to desertification.[15] One of the causes of the war in Darfur, Sudan, relates to environmental degradation and conflict over resources (see chapter 3).

Even if there were no more greenhouse gas emissions from tomorrow, the world will still warm to 1.4°C above the level in pre-industrial times. There are currently around 430 parts per million carbon dioxide equivalent in the atmosphere. If, as seems certain, the level rises to 450 parts per million carbon dioxide equivalent, the probable eventual level of global warming will be between 2 and 3.5°C, with the likeliest rise around 2.5°C. If nothing much changes between now and 2035 (likely on current policies), there will then be 550 parts per million in the atmosphere, with a likely temperature rise of 3.5°C.

These highly probable levels of warming will bring dramatic environmental changes, which will create enormous problems for the world. If, as seems certain, the level of global warming is eventually 2°C above pre-industrial times, this will result in increased water scarcity for between 0.4 billion and 1.7 billion people. This level of warming will therefore very likely produce environmentally driven migration and exacerbate conflicts over resources. US intelligence believes 'climate change is unlikely to trigger interstate war, but it could lead to increasingly heated interstate recriminations and possibly to low-level armed conflicts'.[16]

However, if the world warms by 3.5°C or more, then the prospects are much worse, though the reader can be thankful they will be unlikely to be alive to witness their full realization. A major redrawing of the world map due to rising sea levels, major species extinctions, and a global fall in food production are all likely prospects. For example, a study in the US journal *Science* found half the world's population could face severe food shortages by the end of the century due to falling food production.[17] The full effects may not be felt for many decades, but the trends will start to become noticeable in our lifetimes, with likely disastrous consequences for human well-being and security.

For example, the United Nations Development Programme states: 'climate change is the defining human development challenge of the 21st century. Failure to respond to that challenge will stall and then reverse international efforts to reduce poverty. The poorest countries and most vulnerable citizens will suffer the earliest and most damaging setbacks, even though they have contributed least to the problem'.[18]

The second, related, security threat is increasing competition over resources. Climate change will very likely reduce the 'productivity' of the world, leading to fewer resources. Unfortunately, even before this happens, humanity is already living beyond its means. According to the *Living Planet Report 2008*, 'humanity's demand on the planet's living resources, its Ecological Footprint, now exceeds the planet's regenerative capacity by about 30 per cent. This global overshoot is growing and, as a consequence, ecosystems are being run down and waste is accumulating in the air, land and water. The resulting deforestation, water shortages, declining biodiversity, and climate change are putting the well-being and development of all nations at increasing risk'.[19] This problem will worsen, as the world's population is increasing rapidly. It is projected to increase about 30 per cent by 2035.

As a result, the US National Intelligence Council projects that the number of people suffering inadequate water supplies will increase from 600 million people in 21 countries today to 1,400 million people in 36 countries in 2025.[20] Increasing competition over a share of a shrinking cake is a sure recipe for conflict. Water, essential for human life and agriculture, and oil, essential for a modern industrial economy, are the two resources most likely to provoke tensions that could lead to major armed conflicts in the years ahead.[21]

The third security threat is the marginalization of the majority of the world's population. The world is already a highly unequal place, with the majority of the world excluded from the material benefits and opportunities readers of this book have long taken for granted. As Chris Abbott, Paul Rogers and John

Sloboda of the Oxford Research Group point out, 'globally, more than 1 billion people must try to survive on less than $1 a day, and almost half of the world's 2.2 billion children live in poverty... almost 2 billion people live in countries where regimes do not fully accommodate civil and political freedoms'.[22] According to the UN there are 963 million people, 14 per cent of the world's population, suffering from hunger.[23]

In contrast, as Rogers writes, the 'trans-global élite community [is comprised] of about 1.2 billion people, mainly in the countries of the Atlantic community and the West Pacific, but with élite communities in the tens of millions in countries such as China, India and Brazil'.

The world has always been an unequal place, but in the last 20 years the revolution in communications, brought about largely by the emergence of the internet and satellite television, has meant that those who are marginalized are now keenly aware that they are.

The fundamental injustices of the international order must be readily apparent to the marginalized. As Paul Rogers has written of the 2008-09 global financial crisis, 'the prospects for poorer communities rarely loom large in the recovery policies of the world's wealthy states. Such behavior has reached almost grotesque proportions in the current crisis, with wealthy states willing to commit more than a trillion dollars to rescue their own banking system in crisis. These are financial outlays that are enormous when compared with those that are being committed to achieving the United Nations Millennium Development Goals'.

The rich countries of the West are principally responsible for the carbon emissions and related adverse climate impacts that will have greatest impact on the developing world. As Paul Rogers writes, 'some of the most fragile of the world's economies... will suffer most from... the impact of climate change. More generally, the bitterness that already exists across continents will be reinforced by a perception that the dominant economies have little or no interest in the majority of the world's people'.[24] US Intelligence agrees: 'increasing interconnectedness will enable individuals to coalesce around common causes across national boundaries, creating new cohorts of the angry, downtrodden and disenfranchised'.[25]

Climate change and the resulting increasing competition for scarcer resources will worsen the plight of those already marginalized, and this cocktail will likely breed increasing resentment, political instability and political violence in the years ahead.

This analysis is, of course, very different from the discussion of security issues found in much of the media. Events like the massacre in Mumbai in late 2008, or the possibility of groups like al-Qaeda acquiring weapons of mass destruction, dominate the discussion of security issues in the media. But terrorism, though high profile, affects and kills relatively few people. It is a symptom, not a cause of conflict.

As far as analyzing the likely drivers of conflict is concerned, however, the British Government largely agrees with the analysis above. *The National Security Strategy of the United Kingdom*, published in 2008, identifies 'drivers of insecurity'. It says 'climate change is potentially the greatest challenge to global stability and security... the direct effects are likely to fall most heavily on those countries least able to deal with them, and therefore most likely both to suffer humanitarian disaster but also to tip into instability, state failure or conflict'.[26] On competition for resources, it focuses on energy, saying 'competition for energy [has]... potentially serious security implications. Along with climate change and water stress, it is one of the biggest potential drivers of the breakdown of the rules-based international system and the re-emergence of major inter-state conflict, as well as increasing regional tensions and instability'. On marginalization, it notes 'poverty, inequality, lack of economic development and opportunity, and poor governance are all highly correlated with insecurity and instability, both in individual countries and across regions'.

The strategy also accepts that the interaction of these factors will deliver instability and violence: 'the complex and unpredictable interaction of those multiple stresses will increase the pressure on social, economic, and political structures, particularly in those countries least able to cope, and therefore most likely to tip into instability, conflict or state failure'.

The relevance of traditional 'national defense'

How are governments reacting to the security implications of the trends identified above? As the British American Security Information Council (BASIC) has written, 'the UK defense posture can be summed up as having the capability to mount full-scale military interventions alongside the United States, against nations considered a threat against vital interests'.[27] Such a statement could equally apply to the US and the European Union (EU). Frequently, as with Afghanistan, such operations will involve intervening in a pre-existing conflict. This is the 'security' response to the trends identified above.

Such a stance demands the maintenance of a large arms industry. It represents the prioritizing of an investment in dealing by military force with the problems caused by climate change, scarcer resources and marginalization. The US Government, for example, spends 18 times more on the military compared with spending on policies to counteract the trends identified. While the US in Fiscal Year 2009 will spend $549 billion on the military, it will spend just $1.66 billion on energy efficiency and renewable energy vital to the fight against climate change.[28] Inevitably, a large

Climate change, conflict and political instability

The countries that, due to climate change, are at a high risk of conflict or political instability are listed below.

High risk of conflict

Afghanistan
Algeria
Angola
Bangladesh
Bolivia
Bosnia &
  Herzegovina
Burma
Burundi
Central African
  Republic
Chad
Colombia
Congo
Côte d'Ivoire
Democratic
  Republic of
  Congo
Djibouti
Eritrea
Ethiopia
Ghana
Guinea
Guinea Bissau
Haiti
India
Indonesia
Iran
Iraq
Israel &
  Occupied
  Territories
Jordan
Lebanon
Liberia
Nepal
Nigeria
Pakistan

Peru
Philippines
Rwanda
Senegal
Sierra Leone
Solomon
  Islands
Somalia
Somaliland
Sri Lanka
Sudan
Syria
Uganda
Uzbekistan
Zimbabwe

High risk of political instability

Albania
Armenia
Azerbaijan
Belarus
Brazil
Cambodia
Cameroon
Comoros
Cuba
Dominican
  Republic
Ecuador
Egypt
El Salvador
Equatorial
  Guinea
Fiji
Gambia
Georgia
Guatemala
Guyana
Honduras
Jamaica
Kazakhstan
Kenya
Kiribati
Kyrgyzstan
Laos
Libya
Macedonia
Maldives
Mali
Mauritania
Mexico
Moldova
Montenegro
Morocco
Niger

North Korea
Papua New
  Guinea
Russia
Saudi Arabia
Serbia (Kosovo)
South Africa
Taiwan
Tajikistan
Thailand
Timor-Leste
Togo
Tonga
Trinidad and
  Tobago
Turkey
Turkmenistan
Ukraine
Vanuatu
Venezuela
Western Sahara
Yemen

Source: A Climate of Conflict, International Alert (http://www.international-alert.org/pdf/A_Climate_Of_Conflict.pdf) accessed 15 November 2008.

arms industry will need an international arms market to sell its wares, to boost revenues and profits, and to reduce costs for the military budgets of the producing countries.

A vicious cycle is being created. Very little investment is being made to counter the key trends which will drive the level of violence in the international system this century. Instead, massive investments continue to be made in the products of the arms industry, so that the symptoms of the world's problems can be dealt with violently. With little action to counter the adverse trends, the demand from governments and paramilitary groups for the increasingly destructive weapons the arms industry produces is bound to increase, meaning political violence will become a permanent and widespread feature of the 21st-century world. The arms industry and the arms trade are a fundamental part of the problem of global insecurity.

But, even on their own terms, such policies are doomed to failure. The nature of conflict has changed so much that the military-industrial complex, built for 'industrial' war, looks increasingly expensive and irrelevant. The unprecedented use of military firepower by the US in Korea and Vietnam led to stalemate and defeat respectively. The Iraq War will, at a conservative estimate, cost the US around $3 trillion and the rest of the world possibly the same amount.[29] As has been readily apparent for some time to many observers, the Iraq War is unlikely to produce beneficial outcomes for the world. As Paul Rogers has argued, it will actually undermine the global fight against terrorism, for 'the immense value of the American occupation of Iraq to al-Qaeda is that it is providing a remarkably effective jihadist combat training zone for a substantial new generation of paramilitaries'.[30] Had $3 trillion instead been spent on action against climate change, and on aid for the developing world, the prospects for this century would already be much brighter.

In short, on current trends, while great swathes of humanity will suffer, and governments fail to deliver sustainable security, the manufacturers and merchants of death will continue to profit.

1 Rupert Smith, *The Utility of Force: The Art of War in the Modern World*, Penguin, 2006. **2** *Shooting Down the MDGs: How irresponsible arms transfers undermine development goals*, Oxfam, Oct 2008. **3** *SIPRI Yearbook 2007*, Appendix 2A. **4** *Human Security Brief 2007*, Simon Fraser University Canada, 2007. **5** Lotta Harbom, Erik Melander & Peter Wallensteen, 'Dyadic Dimensions of Armed Conflict, 1946-2007', in *Journal of Peace Research*, vol 45, no 5, 2008. **6** Paul Collier, 'War and military expenditure in developing countries and their consequences for development', in *The Economics of Peace and Security Journal*, vol 1, no 1, 2006. **7** See footnote 4. **8** See footnote 3. **9** *SIPRI Yearbook 2008*, chapter 2. **10** See footnote 9. **11** See footnote 4. **12** Lotta Harbom, Erik Melander & Peter Wallensteen, 'Dyadic Dimensions of Armed Conflict, 1946-2007', in *Journal of Peace Research*, vol 45, no 5, 2008. **13** I am indebted for much of this section to the published analyses of the Oxford Research Group. **14** Much of the information about climate change is taken from Gabrielle Walker and Sir David King, *The Hot Topic: How To Tackle Global Warming And Still Keep the Lights On*, Bloomsbury, 2008. **15** Chris Abbott, Paul Rogers & John Sloboda, *Beyond Terror: The Truth About the Real Threats to Our World*, Rider, 2007. **16** US National Intelligence Council, *Global Trends 2025: A Transformed World*, US Government Printing Office, Nov 2008). **17** *The Guardian*, 9 Jan 2009. **18** http://hdr.undp.org/en/reports/global/hdr2007-2008/ **19** *Living Planet Report 2008*, World Wildlife Fund, Zoological Society of London, Global Footprint Network, 2008. **20** See footnote 16. **21** See footnote 15. **22** See footnote 15. **23** *The Guardian*, 10 Dec 2008. **24** Paul Rogers, *The Financial Crisis and Sustainable Security*, Oxford Research Group, Sep 2008. **25** See footnote 16. **26** Cabinet Office, *The National Security Strategy of the United Kingdom*, The Stationery Office, Mar 2008, chapter 3. **27** Paul Dunne, Samuel Perlo-Freeman, and Paul Ingram, *The real cost behind Trident Replacement and the Carriers*, BASIC, Oct 2007. **28** Miriam Pemberton and Lawrence Korb, *A Unified Security Budget for the United States, FY 2009*, Foreign Policy in Focus, Sep 2008. **29** Joseph Stiglitz and Linda Blimes, *The Three Trillion Dollar War: The True Cost of the Iraq Conflict*, Allen Lane, 2008. **30** Paul Rogers, *The Value of the Iraq War to the Al-Qaida Movement*, Jun 2007, http://tinyurl.com/cfcerq

2 The global arms trade

A picture of the trade, and the countries and companies that are the main players... Who buys and who sells?... Licensed production and the arms trade in international relations.

THE BUSINESS OF buying and selling arms has changed hugely over the last 25 years. For most of the 20th century, right up until the final years of the Cold War, arms companies were essentially national assets in the NATO or Warsaw Pact countries manufacturing weapons systems, arms and other equipment to meet domestic needs.

The companies were intimately involved in the military ambitions of their host country. They were often state-owned, usually inseparable from the country's own armed forces, and strategically connected to their host country's international, national and military enterprises.

During the Cold War from 1947 to 1989, military expenditure grew rapidly to new heights. As the Stockholm International Peace Research Institute (SIPRI) notes, 'more economic resources were used for military purposes after World War Two than ever before; during the 1980s, the level of world military spending was more than 10 times higher than in the period 1925-38'. Demand from the developing world meant 'arms imports by developing countries increased greatly, especially during the 1970s'.

The majority of overseas arms transfers were either sold or donated to strategic partners drawn along Cold War lines. As SIPRI has said, 'demand from the developing world for arms imports during the Cold War was mostly fueled by conflicts, but aspirations for the status of a regional power and the domestic status of the military were also important factors'.[1]

The global arms trade

The chief motivation for the sellers was to lengthen local production lines and so reduce the unit cost of the weapons for the seller government.

For the most part, states paid for and carried out military research themselves and awarded contracts to domestic arms companies to meet mainly their own military needs and those of their allies.

With the strengthening of alliances in the Cold War environment, a few cross-border weapons manufacturing projects were undertaken. Britain and France built the Jaguar strike plane in the 1970s, and Britain, Germany and Italy linked up to build the Tornado jet fighter in the 1980s.

But political implications, worries over national security and secrecy, and other practical problems stalled many projects for decades and stopped others in their early stages. An example is the Eurofighter Typhoon jet fighter program, launched in 1985, but not entering into service until the first decade of the 21st century. Another is the Joint Strike Fighter (JSF), where there is a dispute over US reluctance to transfer critical technical knowledge about the aircraft to Britain.

The end of Cold War tensions in the late 1980s, and the collapse of the USSR, greatly changed the

---

Whose figures for military expenditure?

The arms trade is a notoriously secretive business: not surprisingly, given that countries want to protect their national security by keeping hidden the details of what they buy from potential future enemies.

In addition, the pricing of weapons and weapons systems varies according to currency fluctuations, commissions, off-set arrangements and profit margins. Of course, it also depends on who is giving you the figures.

As a result it is virtually impossible to compile accurate statistics on the military expenditure of one country, let alone worldwide. For the purposes of continuity, figures for military expenditure for countries and worldwide in this chapter are taken as recorded by SIPRI, which has an excellent reputation and consistent research methods. ∎

Source: SIPRI Arms Transfer Database www.sipri.org/contents/armstrad/at_db.html accessed 7 November 2008.

The international arms trade since 1987

Volume of imports of major conventional weapons 1987-2007.

Figures are trend-indicator* values, expressed in millions of US dollars at constant (1990) prices.

Year	Value	Year	Value	Year	Value
1987	39,409	1994	22,545	2001	18,677
1988	36,158	1995	22,347	2002	16,759
1989	34,178	1996	23,544	2003	18,750
1990	29,887	1997	28,105	2004	21,089
1991	27,701	1998	27,026	2005	21,256
1992	24,165	1999	23,997	2006	26,223
1993	26,351	2000	18,278	2007	24,210

The SIPRI data on arms transfers refer to actual deliveries of major conventional weapons. To permit comparison between the data on such deliveries of different weapons and identification of general trends, SIPRI uses a 'trend indicator value'. The SIPRI values are only an indicator of the volume of international arms transfers and not the actual financial value of such transfers. ∎

world arms market. There was a large reduction in the global demand for military equipment. Between 1989 and 1998, global military expenditure fell by one third, with the steepest reduction in the former USSR and Warsaw Pact countries. Military spending in Africa, the Americas and Western Europe also declined.

This had a big impact on the arms trade. SIPRI records that the global volume of military imports of major conventional weapons, such as planes, tanks and explosive systems was, at constant 1990 prices, $18,278 million in 2000, compared with $22,347 million in 1995 and $39,409 million in 1987.

Since the 11 September 2001 terrorist attacks on the US, the 'war on terror' has given a shot in the arm to the international arms trade. It has increased around 30 per cent since 2001, driven by large increases in global military spending. Between 1998 and 2007, global military spending increased by 45 per cent in real terms.[2]

The global arms trade

An international business

Like industries in many other fields, the arms industry has become 'globalized'. This has occurred over several decades.[3]

The huge costs of modern military equipment mean that the arms industry has undergone a process of consolidation and rationalization in most countries. This could be seen as far back as the 1960s when the British Government backed Rolls Royce taking over Bristol Siddeley to become the sole manufacturer of military jet engines in Britain. British Aerospace (BAe) was born in 1977 as a nationalized company resulting from a merger between several different arms companies.

The end of the Cold War accelerated this trend. The US had over 50 major arms companies in the early 1980s, but only five by the end of the 1990s. In Britain BAe acquired the military parts of GEC/Marconi and other arms companies such as submarine builder VSEL. This made the newly named BAE Systems (BAES) the only company in Britain making major weapons systems.

The arms industry has been forced to consolidate across international boundaries. In the 1960s and 1970s international companies had been formed from companies in different countries: Panavia (makers of the Tornado fighter aircraft) and SNECMA (makers of jet engines) are two examples. Recent years have seen the creation of companies like the European Aeronautic Defence and Space Company (EADS), which was created from German, French and Spanish companies.

The dramatic growth of US military spending since 11 September 2001 has led to many arms companies attempting to access the US market by buying American companies. So BAES bought United Defense Corporation in 2005 and Armor Holdings in 2007, QinetiQ bought two US aerospace and military companies in 2004 and 2005, and VT Group bought the Cube Corporation in 2005.[4] In Europe, EADS and Thales also bought US companies. Despite being seen as a 'British' company, BAES now generates more revenue from US military procurement than it does from Britain.

Several other trends have been driving the internationalization of the arms trade.[5]

The emphasis of the so-called Revolution in Military Affairs is on high-technology weapons controlled by sophisticated information technology systems. Arms companies have increasingly become integrators of commercial off-the-shelf products into military hardware. So some civil sector companies, not traditionally part of arms production, have now become major military suppliers, as many mainstream technologies are now effectively 'dual use'. As the Control Arms campaign has pointed out, arms companies 'use commercially available components sourced from highly globalized civilian industries. For example, digital signal processors used in the latest DVD players can also be found in guidance/target acquisition systems for fighter jet missile systems, and microwave chip technology used in Hellfire missiles and Apache Longbow attack helicopters is also found in satellite TV dishes and mobile phones'.

Many governments have opened up their procurement procedures, allowing arms companies from all over the world to bid in open competition for contracts. This process has forced down profit margins, forcing arms companies to behave like other global companies, sourcing components from where technology is best or costs lowest. So, as Control Arms has pointed out, the Ukrainian company Kharkiv Morozov uses components from Italy and the US to make armored personnel carriers, while Singapore Technologies Kinetics, in a joint venture with Turkish company Otokar, uses US engines and transmissions to make armored vehicles. Increasingly, developing countries are offering improved manufacturing and promoting themselves as assemblers of high technology equipment for major Western arms companies.

This has produced what Dr Steven Schofield has called 'an international hierarchy of arms production', with a few major US arms companies increasingly dominating the most modern high-tech equipment based on massive US budgets. While the top five arms companies had 22 per cent of the arms sales market in 1990, they had 44 per cent of it by 2003.[6]

In the second tier are other suppliers who are subcontractors, or making cheaper, lower-tech weapons. So, as Control Arms says, the number of the top 100 arms companies who are based in countries that have not traditionally been arms exporters has more than doubled since 1990. At the low-tech end of the spectrum there were in 2006, says Control Arms, some 92 countries producing small arms and 76 manufacturing small arms ammunition.

The globalization of arms production is increasing technology transfers and enabling sophisticated arms production capabilities to be attained by more and more countries. Eurocopter, a subsidiary of EADS, has played a key role in technology transfer to China, India, South Africa and Korea and has 20 subsidiary companies on six continents.

The result of globalization can be seen by looking at arms fairs. At the French arms fair Eurosatory the number of exhibiting companies from outside Europe rose from two in 1992 to over 290 in 2008. At the annual arms fair IDEX held in the United Arab Emirates, the number of companies from the Asia Pacific region exhibiting more than doubled between 1999 and 2006.

Yet arms manufacturers necessarily remain in close collusion with states. Their products are still national assets, and their only customers are governments.

Governments still use their arms industries as a diplomatic tool in international relations, granting arms deals with other governments as part of wider agreements.

Thus the arms trade, as it appears today, is unique in terms of international business – its companies are still jealously treasured as national assets by the countries from which they sprang, receiving special treat-

---

Not just things that go 'bang'

There is a common misconception that the arms trade is all about the buying and selling of things that go 'bang'. It is about planes like Hawk, Harrier and Tornado; it involves selling heat-seeking missiles, armed warheads and bombs; it is about armored tanks and submarines; and it is about guns, rifles, rocket launchers and grenades. But the trade in military *matériel* is also about components: the nuts and bolts, the metal panels and the plastic switches, the wheels and electronics that make the systems work.

This is significant since, as Control Arms points out, 'the export of military components is an ever-increasing part of the global arms market... weapons systems are now, more than ever, assembled from components sourced from a global market place'.[7] For example, their analysis of British Government annual reports on arms exports covering 1998 to 2002 showed an eleven-fold increase in the number of licenses granted for components over this period. This raises a number of problems, for example monitoring the end-use of components is clearly more difficult than monitoring complete weapons systems. Equally, as in the ALH case (see page 31), components can be exported for incorporation into weapons systems in countries which have less effective export controls.

Part of the industry is about the trade in information and technology – weapons design, knowledge and engineering skill. In some licensed production deals, no hardware is exchanged at all – merely the license to produce a weapons system, and the instruction manual on how to build and use it. Prison and policing equipment – riot shields, handguns, CS gas, truncheons, water cannon, armored vehicles – are also part of the arms business. As if all this were not enough, the trade includes the buying and selling of sheer human might – it is about mercenaries, or private armies. Whether the hiring of private armies is to supplement a country's armed forces or fight off rebels, to defend a lucrative diamond mine, or to overthrow a dictator, it is still part of the dirty business. ∎

ment, political and financial support. Yet in almost every other respect they function exactly like other large transnational corporations.

Blurring the boundaries: licensed production

In *The Arms Industry*, Chris Wrigley notes: 'the simple concept of an arms company disappears into a labyrinth of licensed production, joint ventures, conglomerates, strategic partnerships, and Co-operative Armament Programs. The concept of arms trade becomes equally elusive. When weapons 'systems' may be designed in one country, manufactured piecemeal in several others and sold both to the collaborating states and to others, what is an export and who is the exporter? Indeed, what are arms, when a harmless Land Rover vehicle may be sold or licensed to a semi-respectable government and turn up later, equipped with armor, radio and machine-guns, in the service of a distinctly disreputable one?'

As we are beginning to see, the arms trade has never really been about one arms company in one country selling a single weapons system to another country's government in exchange for a fat check. The arms trade is much more of a complex web, and campaigning against it is more complicated than at first appears.

One of the clearest examples of the complexity of arms deals, and a classic demonstration of how unscrupulous arms dealers and firms will gratuitously exploit loopholes in pursuit of a fast profit, is the problem of licensed production.

At its simplest, licensed production entails the vendor corporation supplying ready-to-assemble parts with instructions, like a child's modeling kit, to another country which puts it together. At the other end of the scale, the vendor will supply technology and expertise – even expert engineers – and the buying country manufactures the system from scratch.

Licensed production is of concern because it blurs the boundaries of export licensing procedures. When a weapons system is exported from most states, the manufacturer has to apply for permission (an export license) to export it to another country. Permission is granted according to whatever criteria the exporting country might set.

But many countries have no specific export licensing procedures for equipment and technology intended for licensed production. A gaping hole is left in the ability to control arms exports.

In the same way, the export of technology, expertise and information can be more dangerous than exporting the system itself. First, there can be no guarantee that the purchasing company will not continue to produce its own brand of the product, even if this was not provided for in the original contract.

Second, once a country is manufacturing its own arms there can be few restrictions on its selling on those arms, at a profit, to other nations which would not have been allowed to buy from the country where the system was originally designed.

For example, the Advanced Light Helicopter (ALH) is made in India by Hindustan Aeronautics Limited.[8] It is a collaborative effort with the German company Eurocopter Deutschland, and involves at least 29 companies in nine countries across four continents. Foreign components imported into India to make the ALH include engines, rotor blades, hydraulics, cockpit displays, rocket launchers and machine guns.

Press reports in 2006 indicated that India was considering selling the ALH to the Burmese military junta. The EU has had an arms embargo on Burma since 1988. Following a report published by various European NGOs drawing attention to the possibility that the ALH could be sold to Burma by India, a respected industry journal reported that 'intense diplomatic and commercial pressure' prevented the

The global arms trade

sale going ahead, even though there was no legal barrier to the sale.[9]

Who sells the weaponry?

Unsurprisingly, the West dominates the world arms market in terms of sales. Over the five-year period 2003-07, the US and Russia towered over the other countries in weapons sales, clocking up $62,881

Big hitters

The top 20 suppliers of major conventional weapons from 2003 to 2007. Figures are trend-indicator values (see box, page 25), expressed in $millions at constant (1990) prices.

Rank 2003-2007	Supplier	2003	2005	2007	2003-2007
1	USA	5581	7026	7454	34499
2	Russia	5355	5576	4588	28382
3	Germany	1707	1879	3395	10889
4	France	1313	1688	2690	9544
5	Britain	624	871	1151	4766
6	Netherlands	342	611	1355	4101
7	Italy	311	818	562	2596
8	Sweden	468	536	413	2141
9	China	580	271	355	2057
10	Ukraine	397	308	109	1731
11	Spain	158	133	529	1701
12	Israel	309	280	238	1635
13	Canada	276	206	343	1337
14	Switzerland	120	196	211	952
15	Poland	72	17	135	522
16	Uzbekistan	340	4		514
17	South Korea	104	32	214	450
18	South Africa	43	24	80	358
19	Belgium	15	171	10	301
20	Denmark	59	1	5	238

million worth (at 1990 prices) between 2003 and 2007. The US sold slightly more ($34,499 million) than Russia ($28,382 million). Their nearest competitors, France and Germany, had sales worth $20,433 million over the same period.

According to SIPRI, just over half (56 per cent) of all transfers (imports) of major conventional weapons between 2003 and 2007 came from the US and Russia. Germany and France accounted for 10 per cent and 9 per cent respectively, with Britain and the Netherlands next with 4 per cent each. The eight following biggest sellers – Italy, Sweden, China, Ukraine, Spain, Israel, Canada and Switzerland – accounted for around 13 per cent of the world's total transfers between them.

So it is clear that the global arms market is controlled by just a few players. The five biggest arms-selling countries – four of whom, ironically, are permanent members of the UN Security Council, whose primary responsibility is the maintenance of international peace and security – accounted for 79 per cent of all arms transfers over that five-year period.

Within those countries, and across their borders, stretch a handful of huge armament companies and hundreds of very small components and specialist manufacturers.

The biggest arms corporations originated in the US, and still call North America home. Those that started operations in Europe are less tied to their country of birth – but remain distinctly European.

The big hitters' world ranking fluctuates from year to year, and accurate statistics are difficult to obtain and compare. The industry website www.defensenews.com shows, however, that the US Lockheed Martin company led the field in terms of sales, with $38.5 billion of sales during 2007. Military equipment made up around 92 per cent of the company's sales in that year.

Boeing is its closest local military equipment manu-

Military might

The top 10 largest arms companies, in terms of military sales. The figures in *italics* represent the percentage of arms in total sales for each company. Figures for arms sales are in $billions. Currency conversions for non-US firms calculated using prevailing rates at the end of each firm's fiscal year.

	2002	2003	2004	2005	2006	2007
Lockheed Martin	23.3 *88*	30.1 *95*	34.1 *96*	34.2 *98*	36.1 *91*	38.5 *92*
Boeing	22.0 *41*	27.4 *54*	30.5 *58*	29.2 *56*	30.8 *50*	32.1 *48*
BAE Systems	15.0 *77*	17.2 *77*	20.3 *80*	20.9 *79*	25.1 *93*	29.8 *95*
Northrop Grumman	12.3 *71*	18.7 *71*	22.1 *74*	23.3 *76*	23.7 *78*	24.6 *77*
General Dynamics	9.8 *71*	12.8 *77*	15.0 *78*	16.6 *78*	18.8 *78*	21.5 *79*
Raytheon	15.3 *91*	16.9 *93*	18.8 *93*	18.2 *83*	19.5 *96*	19.8 *93*
EADS	6.3 *20*	8.0 *21*	10.5 *24*	9.1 *23*	13.2 *25*	12.2 *21*
L-3 Communications	3.6 *89*	4.4 *86*	6.1 *89*	8.5 *91*	10.0 *80*	11.2 *81*
Finmeccanica	3.9 *48*	5.9 *54*	7.7 *60*	7.1 *56*	9.1 *55*	10.6 *54*
United Technologies	3.6 *13*	5.3 *17*	6.7 *18*	6.8 *16*	7.7 *16*	8.8 *16*

facturing competitor, but the company itself is much larger – weapons sales made up only 48 per cent of total sales in 2007. According to www.defensenews. com, BAES was the third largest arms seller in 2007, with $29.8 billion in weapons sales – almost all (95 per cent) of its business.

The other major league weapons producers are the American companies Northrop Grumman, General Dynamics and Raytheon and the European company EADS.

Who buys the weapons?

It is when one glances at the list of the main purchasers of weapons that the problem of the arms trade really begins to emerge. The top 20 arms importers in recent years, according to SIPRI, include human-rights abusing states like Turkey and China; and countries in areas of military tension such as South Korea, India, Greece, Israel and Pakistan. Different countries do, of course, have traditional suppliers, often as a hangover from Cold War alliances.

China, India, the United Arab Emirates, Greece and South Korea were the biggest importers of arms

Buying firepower

The top 20 arms-purchasing countries between 2003 and 2007. Figures are trend-indicator values (see box, page 25), expressed in $millions at constant (1990) prices.

Rank 2003-2007	Recipient	2003	2005	2007	2003-2007
1	China	2068	3346	1424	13463
2	India	2870	1182	1318	9105
3	UAE	700	2224	1040	7467
4	Greece	2226	540	2089	7170
5	South Korea	575	661	1807	5536
6	Israel	292	1108	891	4239
7	Egypt	816	736	418	3743
8	Australia	864	560	685	3432
9	Turkey	433	984	944	2853
10	USA	501	476	587	2601
11	Pakistan	592	333	715	2347
12	Chile	175	403	615	2283
13	Japan	465	299	519	2171
14	Poland	376	97	985	2123
15	Britain	787	16	698	1969
16	Italy	516	136	176	1965
17	Taiwan	101	794	3	1846
18	Singapore	70	543	707	1751
19	South Africa	2	187	855	1734
20	Spain	110	391	385	1669

over the last five years. But recent studies by the Congressional Research Service on behalf of the US Congress reveal that arms sales to developing nations have far outweighed arms sales to developed countries since the turn of the century. According to their figures, developing countries accounted for 55.6 per cent of the value of all international arms deliveries in 2007. Between 2004 and 2007, the figure was 64.7 per cent, and in the four years prior to that it was 65.1 per cent.[10]

The arms trade in international relations

Despite the growth of private arms companies from former state-owned firms, the arms business remains inseparable from the political movements of today's world. As alliances are struck between nations and across continents, as agreements are signed and incorporated into domestic legislation, the arms industry plays an important and strategic part. World politics can be compared to a board game, with world leaders as the players and arms companies as their willing pawns. Some argue it is the other way around. There is a blurred boundary between government and corporations (see chapter 6).

Joint weapons programs (via companies such as Panavia, SEPECAT, Eurofighter and Eurocopter) have solidified European alliances.

The so-called 'special relationship' between the US and Britain has also been punctuated by collaborative arms projects, most starkly the JSF, which will produce around 2,400 fighter planes for the US and around 140 for Britain. Total production is currently planned at around 3,100 aircraft.[11] Britain is the only full collaborator in the project, though the Netherlands, Australia, Canada, Denmark, Norway, Italy and Turkey all have lesser stakes in it.[12]

As Chris Wrigley writes in *The Arms Industry*: 'The real point is that the Joint Strike Fighter is essentially a US plane, designed to be the main instrument of US global military hegemony in the next generation. The [British] Royal Navy will have a small share of the output, and so of the hegemony'.[13] The British Government envisages itself as the junior partner in US global hegemony and wants the arms industry to adapt accordingly. The Defence Industrial Strategy stated in 2005: 'to exploit this effectively, our Armed Forces need to be interoperable with US command and control structures, match the US operational tempo and provide those capabilities that deliver the greatest impact when operating alongside the US.'

The EU and the arms industry[14]

It is certainly the intention of the main European states to smooth arms purchasing between themselves and to improve joint working, thereby strengthening Europe as a region in terms of military might, economic independence and political significance. The arms companies have their own interests in growth, allegiances and market share.

The EU wants to create a credible European Defense Identity, which would include an effective European arms industry, producing the weapons Europe wants at a lower cost than if each EU member had its own arms industries.

In 2004 the European Defense Agency (EDA) was created to promote coherence in European military procurement and encourage the development of pan-European military production and collaboration. In 2006 it published its 'Initial Long-Term Vision For European Defense Capability And Capacity Needs'. This envisaged the EU conducting 'expeditionary, multinational and multi-instrument' operations, aimed at 'achieving security and stability more than "victory"'. The report warned that the US is outspending Europe six to one in military Research and Development (R&D) and that unless Europe invested more in the arms industry 'the trends points towards a steady contraction of the European defense industry into niche producers working increasingly for US primes'. It advocated 'overcoming the notorious fragmentation of the European defense industrial scene', demanding 'redoubled efforts' to consolidate.[15]

In response to the consolidation of the US arms industry described earlier, the creation of companies such as EADS and Thales has started the process of creating a European arms industry more quickly than had been anticipated. Even so, in 2005 there were still 89 major weapons programs in the EU (including 23 national programs for armored fighting vehicles) compared with 27 in the US.[16]

Several initiatives have been taken to consolidate the EU's arms industry. The Organisation Conjoint de Coopération en matière d'Armement (OCCAR), established in 1996 is a joint procurement program to which Belgium, Britain, France, Germany, Italy and Spain belong. So far it has concluded an 18-billion-Euro contract for the Airbus military transport A400M. Other OCCAR projects are for a combat helicopter, missile systems, vehicles and radar systems.

In 2000, six European nations (Britain, France, Germany, Italy, Spain and Sweden) finalized details of an agreement to smooth arms purchasing and weapons manufacturing collaboration between them, called the Framework Agreement.

The Agreement outlined common research, development and supply of joint weapons projects between the signatory countries. But it also established protocols for exporting those weapons outside the group of six. Campaigners lobbied against the Agreement, arguing that it would reduce transparency and accountability of arms exports from member countries.

Under the Framework Agreement, signatories collaborating on an arms project draw up a list of countries to which they wish to export the system. The list is not open to scrutiny by elected parliamentarians in the member states, let alone the general public. Also, arms export licensing procedures only apply from the country on whose soil the weapons or components are manufactured and exported, not under the export rules of every collaborating member – the process in place before the Agreement was established. A similar agreement has been established between the Nordic countries: Denmark, Finland, Norway and Sweden. This has been followed up by a proposal to 'facilitate the circulation of defense-related products within the EU-internal market' agreed by the European Parliament in December 2008.

It is easy for our eyes to glaze over when confronted by details like those in this chapter – arms corporations with bewildering acronyms, weapons systems with daunting names. But the reason we need to pay attention is that this particular kind of business activity must be measured in terms not just of money but of its overwhelmingly negative impact on conflict, human rights and development – on life and death.

1 *SIPRI Yearbook 2006.* **2** *SIPRI Yearbook 2008.* **3** Much of the information in this section is taken from Steven Schofield, *Making Arms, Wasting Skills*, Campaign Against Arms Trade, Apr 2008. **4** *SIPRI Yearbook 2006.* **5** Much of the information in this section is taken from *Arms Without Borders*, Control Arms Campaign, Oct 2006. **6** See footnote 4. **7** *Lock, Stock and Barrel: How British Arms Components Add up to Deadly Weapons*, Control Arms Campaign, Feb 2004. **8** Much of the information in this section is taken from *Indian helicopters for Myanmar: making a mockery of embargoes?*, Amnesty International UK and Saferworld, Jul 2007. **9** Amnesty International, *Blood at the Crossroads: Making the case for a global Arms Trade Treaty*, 2008. **10** Richard F Grimmett, *Conventional Arms Transfers to Developing Nations, 2000-2007*, Congressional Research Service, 23 Oct 2007. **11** http://tinyurl.com/anyawg. **12** www.jsf.mil/index.htm. **13** Chris Wrigley, *The Arms Industry*, Campaign Against Arms Trade, Mar 2001. **14** Much of the information in this section is taken from Martin Broek and Wendela de Vries, *The Arms Industry and the EU Constitution*, ENAAT, Jan 2006. **15** *An Initial Long-Term Vision For European Defence Capability and Capacity Needs*, European Defence Agency, Oct 2006. **16** See footnote 3.

3 Impact on conflicts

**The boomerang effect... Military training... Examples
of hostilities and their military quartermasters.**

THE ARMS TRADE plays a major part in sustaining
tensions and conflicts both within and between states.
The deadly dealing increases strains and thereby fuels
tensions between nations.

Take the US for example. A report by Frida Berrigan,
William D Hartung and Leslie Heffel showed that in
2006 and 2007, the US transferred $11.2 billion in
arms and military services to 20 war zones. The
biggest recipients were Pakistan ($3.7 billion), Turkey
($3 billion), Israel ($2.1 billion), Iraq ($1.4 billion) and
Colombia ($575 million).

The report concluded: 'US weapons are present
in fully half of the major armed conflicts currently
under way worldwide. And in some potential
conflicts – between India and Pakistan, Pakistan and
Afghanistan, and Turkey and the Kurdish region of
northern Iraq, forces on both sides are receiving US
arms and training'.[1]

The boomerang effect

One of the most frequent arguments that politicians
and arms company executives use to justify the lethal
industry is that weapons help to create stability in the
world. Countries have a right to defend themselves
from attack. When the West is covertly, or openly,
supplying arms to rebel and revolutionary movements that accord with their interests, they argue that
oppressed people have a right to attempt to overthrow
their oppressor and install democracy.

But it is an old saying that your friend today
may become your enemy in the future, and in no
field is this truer than in the world of weaponry.
We in the West may happily arm a country today,

but we cannot predict whether, at some time in the future, we may be facing those very same munitions in a conflict with that country – as happened for example with the Malvinas/Falklands war against Argentina when British forces faced 'friendly' French Exocet missiles. This is a particularly significant point because, as the British Government acknowledged in its *Defence Industrial Strategy*, the immense costs of high-tech weapons mean weapons systems produced and exported today will have very long life-spans.

During the USSR's occupation of Afghanistan, the US and Europe (including Britain) shipped tons of arms to rebels. An estimated 250 to 350 surface-to-air missile launchers (Britain supplied Blowpipe, the US supplied Stinger) were used in the 1980s Afghan conflict. Many of the same Mujahedin-backed rebels who took the Afghan capital in 1996 are known today as the Taliban. Since 2001, the US and Britain have been at war with them, and their estimated remaining 100 Stingers, as part of the 'war on terror'. The World Policy Institute's William Hartung writes: 'small arms almost always outlast the political relationships that existed between the original supplier and recipient, and one needs look no farther than the anti-US activities of Osama bin Laden and his network of former Afghan freedom fighters to see how covert arms sales can come back to haunt the supplier nations'.[2]

Other places where US troops faced adversaries armed with US military hardware include Panama, Iraq, Somalia, and Haiti.

Military training
Military training is an aspect of the industry often overlooked by campaigners and politicians working towards arms control. Yet the provision of training to foreign armies, or warring factions, is commonplace and was clearly illustrated with the allied forces' training and assistance given to the Afghan United Front

forces during their reclaiming of Afghanistan at the end of 2001.

Just as with the hardware, military training is used by governments to further their strategic and political objectives, as well as being a tool in international relations.

Since the US armed forces are among the most highly trained and best financially supported in the world, it is no surprise that the US is a major provider of military training.

In 1998, for example, the US provided $45.8 million in international military education training (IMET) for over 400 African soldiers. Under the Pentagon's Joint Combined Exchange Training (JCET) program, US Special Forces trained military personnel from at least 34 of Africa's 53 nations. That included troops fighting on both sides of the Democratic Republic of the Congo (DRC)'s 'civil' war – from Rwanda and Uganda (supporting the rebels) to Zimbabwe and Namibia (supporting the DRC's Kabila regime).

When Rwandan soldiers invaded the DRC (then called Zaire) in 1996, attacking refugees and massacring civilians, the US was forced to defend its training of Rwandan troops. *The Washington Post* revealed that the troops had received combat training from the US, as well as human rights training.

Lethal Learning
Leading recipients of British military training, 1997-2006

Country	Soldiers trained
Kuwait	1,829
Netherlands	1,526
Canada	1,434
Norway	1,375
Oman	1,135
United Arab Emirates	1,004
Total soldiers trained	24,132
Total countries receiving training	145

Source: Hansard, 10 October 2005.

A more recent example is in Darfur, the scene of a humanitarian disaster. Despite indiscriminate air attacks by the Sudanese Air Force using Russian-supplied aircraft, Russia in 2007 continued to provide training to Sudanese Air Force pilots, according to Amnesty.[3]

That the arms trade fuels war soon becomes clear when you look at the details of particular conflicts, for example those in Darfur, Somalia, Israel and Colombia. For each of the conflicts the arms supplied come from different sources. However, what each example has in common is that the conflict is sustained by large-scale arms transfers to one of the warring sides from a permanent UN Security Council member.

Darfur[4]

Sudan has been an independent nation for 52 years, but has only been at peace for 11. A war between the Government and rebels in southern Sudan ended in 1973 but restarted in 1983. In 1985 the Government started using militias to fight the war in the South, as did the rebel forces. In response the EU imposed an arms embargo in 1994. Both sides, according to Amnesty, 'committed grave human rights abuses'.

Imported weapons were used in the war, with Antonov aircraft and helicopter gunships 'used frequently against civilian targets'. Amnesty notes that between 1996 and 2002 'scores' of indiscriminate attacks were carried out against civilians by the Sudanese Air Force. In 2002 a ceasefire agreement was signed between the Government and the rebels. A Comprehensive Peace Agreement (CPA) was signed in 2005, bringing to an end 20 years of war which had created four million refugees and resulted in the deaths of more than two million people.

However, in recent years international attention has been focused on the Darfur region of Sudan, where another brutal conflict, fueled by imported weapons, has resulted in humanitarian disaster.

Darfur had experienced periods of violence in the late 1970s and early 1980s, between nomads and those who had settled the land. An armed conflict between these groups took place between 1987 and 1989, and tensions continued through the 1990s. The root causes of the Darfur conflict, according to SIPRI, are 'deep political and socio-economic imbalances and the long-term effects of environmental degradation'.[5]

Many of the groups who lived a settled existence felt that Darfur had been sidelined by the Government, and two armed groups, the Sudan Liberation Army (SLA) and the Justice and Equality Movement (JEM), started a rebellion in 2003. The SLA complained of Darfur's marginalization, lack of development, and the failure of the Government to protect the population against armed nomadic groups. The Sudanese Government decided to crush the rebellion by force, and let loose groups of Arab nomadic militia (known as the 'Janjaweed') to help it do so.

Prior to the start of the war in Darfur in 2003, the Sudanese Government had imported weapons from a number of sources. Russia had provided armored personnel carriers; China aircraft, helicopters and small arms; Belarus helicopter gunships, tanks, artillery and vehicles; and France and Iran small arms.

The Janjaweed militia were well armed, driving Land Cruisers, armed with modern communications equipment, and committing atrocities mainly with small arms such as rocket-propelled grenade launchers, AK-47, G3 and FAL rifles. The Janjaweed have received their arms principally from the Sudanese Government – as, effectively, have the rebel groups, who rely largely on captured government supplies. The rebels have also received arms via Chad and Libya.

Amnesty noted that the Sudanese Government, as it did in southern Sudan, in Darfur 'has made extensive use of military aircraft – mainly Antonov military transport aircraft, but also helicopter gunships and MiG jet fighters'. Most of the bombings have been indiscriminate, and often co-ordinated with the Janjaweed militia. Government forces are also reported to have attacked civilians using tanks and artillery.

The flow of imported arms led to a catastrophe for the people of Darfur. Amnesty reported that Sudan's arms suppliers 'have contributed to the capacity of Sudanese leaders to use their army and air force to carry out grave violations of international humanitarian and human rights law. Foreign governments have also enabled the Government of Sudan to arm and deploy untrained and unaccountable militias that have deliberately and indiscriminately killed civilians in Darfur on a large scale, destroying homes, looting property and forcibly displacing the population'. Bombings by the Sudanese Air Force 'had the effect of terrorizing the population and encouraging displacement', with thousands taking refuge in neighboring Chad.

The destruction of Darfur in 2003 and 2004 was 'systematic'. The Janjaweed were responsible for widespread killings, torture and rape.

Partly as a result of the wars in southern Sudan and Darfur, in 2004 Sudan was ranked 139th out of 177 countries in the UN's Human Development Index. At the time, Sudan had the seventh highest military spending in Africa.

In response to the carnage in Darfur, the UN Security Council placed an arms embargo on the Janjaweed and opposition groups in Darfur in July 2004. The exclusion of the Sudanese Government from the embargo and lack of monitoring made it ineffective. In March 2005 the UN Security Council extended the embargo to the Government of Sudan, requiring it to get UN approval before moving military equipment to Darfur.

But in 2006 the UN reported 'blatant violations of the arms embargo by all parties... continue unabated. Weapons, notably small arms, ammunition and military equipment, continue to enter the Darfur states from a number of countries and from the region of the Sudan'. In 2007 the UN again noted 'the ongoing violations of the arms embargo'. Most of Sudan's imports since the embargo have come from two permanent Security Council members – Russia and China.

Since 2005, China has sold arms and ammunition, aircraft and Dong Feng military trucks. In 2008 Amnesty reported that the Janjaweed were mostly armed with weapons of Chinese origin. Russia has exported aircraft, helicopters (including 'Hind' gunships) and Antonov aircraft; Iran has supplied arms and ammunition.

The opposition groups, the SLA and JEM, have also committed grave human rights abuses in Darfur. The UN has claimed that Eritrea has provided them with arms, logistical support and military training, and that JEM has received assault rifles from Chad.

The breaches of the UN arms embargo are serious as the war in Darfur continues to see imported equipment contributing to the dire situation there. In 2007 Amnesty reported that the Sudanese Government was 'continuing to divert and deploy imported attack and other military aircraft, "dual use" and domestically made military equipment, as well as firearms and ammunition... to target civilians directly'.

By 2007, more than 200,000 had died in Darfur, with more than 2.5 million displaced from their homes. Amnesty noted: 'easy access to arms is intensifying and prolonging the conflict with disastrous effects on the civilian population'. It went on: 'the continuing flow of arms, ammunition and related material into the states of north, south and west Darfur... are significant factors contributing to serious human rights violations and abuses'. The conflict is still ongoing.

Somalia[6]

Since 1991, when the dictator Siad Barre was overthrown, Somalia has been torn by civil war. It has been based on clan rivalries, competition over resources, and criminal activity. It has been fueled by arms exports to the warring factions from other countries, with Yemen now the chief source, according to the UN.[7]

In 2004, negotiations finally produced a UN-backed interim Government, but it was opposed by armed Somali groups, including the Islamic Courts Union. The interim Government was in 2006 forced out of the capital Mogadishu and southern Somalia. A military offensive by the interim Government and its backers Ethiopia expelled the Eritrean-backed Islamic Courts Union at the end of 2006.

The 2006 Ethiopian offensive was launched using considerable amounts of imported weapons. According to Amnesty, in 2006 Ethiopia had imported heavy weapons such as tanks and armored vehicles from Russia and China, and in 2005 from North Korea and the Czech Republic. Other military weapons were imported in 2005 and 2006 from China and Israel.

The interim Government, despite the Ethiopian success, faced an armed insurgency from Islamist groups. In 2007 and 2008, insurgent attacks in Mogadishu were met by Ethiopian artillery fire, which sometimes destroyed entire neighborhoods.

Amnesty notes: 'all parties to the conflict in Somalia have continued to commit serious human rights abuses and serious violations of [International Humanitarian Law] despite the 1992 UN arms embargo, and flows of military equipment... from Eritrea, Ethiopia and Yemen have more than likely been used in the recent upsurge in brutal violence on the part of Ethiopian and [interim Government] armed forces and attacks on civilians by armed groups and criminal gangs'. It wrote: 'some 6,000 civilians were reportedly killed in fighting in the capital Mogadishu and across southern and central Somalia in 2007, and over 600,000 Somali civilians were internally displaced from and around Mogadishu'.

The wars make it very difficult for Somalia to develop from its current backward state. As the British Government notes, '60 per cent of Somalia's population lives below the $1 per day poverty line. Human development indicators are uniformly low: only 14 per cent of school age children attend school; Somalia has the worst health indicators in Africa'.[8] And increasingly the instability and chaos brought about by the conflict in Somalia has wider implications.

For instance, the Royal Institute of International Affairs has noted that 'piracy off the coast of Somalia is growing at an alarming rate and threatens to drastically disrupt international trade', with 'one of the most important trade routes in the world... now threatened by the chronic instability in Somalia'. It continues: 'with little functioning government, long, isolated, sandy beaches and a population that is both desperate and used to war, Somalia is a perfect environment for piracy to thrive'.[9]

Israel

In 2000, the 'second intifada' began in the Israeli-occupied territories of the West Bank and Gaza. The territories, invaded by Israel in the war of June 1967, have been under Israeli military occupation since.

The Israeli Defense Forces (IDF) are primarily US-equipped. Amnesty says other significant suppliers to military equipment since 2001 include Australia, Austria, Belgium, the Czech Republic, Finland, Germany, Hungary, Italy, Poland, Romania, Serbia-

Montenegro, Slovakia, Slovenia, South Korea and Spain. The Palestinian Human Rights Monitoring Group estimates that between September 2000, when the Second Intifada began, and 30 November 2008, 6,073 Palestinians were killed by the Israeli security forces[10] (783 Israeli civilians were killed by Palestinians between September 2000 and 28 March 2007[11]).

Since 2000 Israel has received at least $2 billion in military and economic aid every year.[12] In both 2006 and 2007, Israel imported $1 billion in US arms and military equipment through the Foreign Military Sales program.[13] From 2010, the US plans to increase security assistance to Israel from $2.7 billion a year to $3 billion a year over a 10-year period.[14]

During the Second Intifada, the IDF's tactics to counter Palestinian terrorism have included attacks on civilians, extrajudicial executions and home demolitions. Israel has used, say international, Israeli and Palestinian human rights groups, 'disproportionate, excessive, and lethal force'.[15]

Israel attacked the Hizbullah terrorist group in the Lebanon for four days in the summer of 2006. Hundreds of Lebanese civilians were killed and injured and Israeli bombing destroyed much of Lebanon's infrastructure. Cluster bombs, mainly of US origin, were extensively used by Israel. Post-war assessments indicate that there may have been as many as a million unexploded 'bomblets' left on Lebanese soil after the Israeli assault, and these unexploded bomblets have already resulted in around 200 casualties since the conflict ended.[16]

The latest example of Israel's use of its military might is the IDF onslaught on the Gaza Strip which took place over three weeks from 27 December 2008[17]. The Gaza Strip is one of the most densely populated areas of the world, and was in the grip of a humanitarian crisis due to an 18-month Israeli blockade. The IDF attack on Gaza resulted in the deaths of at least

1,300 Palestinians, including more than 300 children, and injured over 5,000. Many of the dead and injured were civilians. Inaccurate attacks on Israel from Palestinian terror groups using crudely made rockets claimed three Israeli lives during the period.

The indiscriminate and disproportionate use of Israeli firepower in one of the most built-up areas in the world is a war crime. As Amnesty has said: 'Put simply, Israel's military intervention in the Gaza Strip has been equipped to a large extent by US-supplied weapons, munitions and military equipment paid for with US taxpayers' money.' Hundreds of homes and lives were destroyed by US-supplied F-16s, bombs and Hellfire missiles as well as anti-tank mines. Particularly cruel (US-supplied) indiscriminate weapons were used by the IDF such as white phosphorous shells which burn 'deeply through muscle and onto the bone, continuing to burn until deprived of oxygen'. Shells filled with flechettes (metal darts designed for maximum wounding effect), designed to be used 'against massed infantry attacks' were also employed in the attack on Gaza, killing civilians.

The rockets of Palestinian terrorists, according to respected military journal *Jane's* are 'inaccurate, short-range and rarely lethal'. Amnesty says that 'most of these rockets fall in empty areas'. Nevertheless, their indiscriminate use is also a war crime.

Prior to the Second Intifada, Britain had sold the IDF small arms and ammunition. Once the Intifada had begun, the IDF were found to be using armored personnel carriers made from Centurion tanks sold to Israel by Britain between 1958 and 1970. This was in breach of assurances given to the British Government that the IDF would not use British-supplied equipment in the Occupied Territories.[18]

US F-16 aircraft have also been used by the IDF in the Occupied Territories. In July 2002, the British Foreign Secretary announced that the export of

British components for Heads-Up-Displays (HUDs) in F-16 aircraft made in the US but sold to Israel would be permitted.[19] HUDs 'greatly facilitate... targeting by fighter aircraft'.[20]

The NGO Saferworld has noted that there appeared to be a tightening of British arms export policy to Israel in 2002 after the breach of assurances by the Israelis was discovered. However, by 2006, the number of licenses granted was back to 2001 levels, and a British Foreign Office Minister had admitted 'almost any piece of equipment... could be used aggressively'. Saferworld notes that 'since the beginning of 2002 the UK has licensed a range of equipment critical for offensive operations'.[21]

While Israel attacked Hezbollah in the Lebanon, the British Government continued to authorize licenses to Israel, as Saferworld pointed out. Licenses were granted for, among other things, armored all-wheel-drive vehicles, components for military helicopters, and components for pilotless air vehicle control equipment (the IDF used pilotless aerial vehicles extensively in Lebanon).[22]

Colombia

There has been a vicious internal war in Colombia since the mid-1960s, when two guerrilla groups – The Revolutionary Armed Forces of Colombia (FARC) and the National Liberation Army (ELN) – were founded. By 2005, the conflict had killed at least 200,000 people and displaced another two million.

According to Amnesty there are 'serious human rights abuses and violations of [International Humanitarian Law] by all parties to the conflict in Colombia'.[23] At least 1,400 people were killed in the internal war in 2007, with hundreds of thousands displaced.

All sides are responsible for the killing of civilians. Amnesty estimates that in 2007 guerrillas killed 260 civilians, the right-wing paramilitary groups (often in collusion with the security forces) killed 300, and Colombia's security forces killed another 330.

Colombia's Industria Militar (INDUMIL) in 2006 was granted the exclusive right to commercialize the Israeli Galil rifle – INDUMIL produces 45,000 every year. Yet Amnesty notes that Colombia still relies heavily on imports. Major suppliers include South Africa (who sold $10 million worth of arms to Colombia in 2007), Israel ($8.7 million) and France ($2.3 million).

Weapons are also imported via a wide range of illicit routes. A UN report has said that illegally imported weapons have come from Europe, China, North Korea, the US and Latin America. Typically these weapons end up in the hands of the paramilitary or guerrilla groups.

The US, however, is the major supplier to the Colombian Government. In 2006 and 2007 the US delivered around $575 million worth of arms through its Foreign Military Sales program.[24] Between 2002 and 2009 Colombia will have received $5.4 billion in military and police aid. Colombia is the fifth largest recipient of US military assistance in the world (after Afghanistan, Iraq, Israel and Egypt).[25]

A study by the Rand Corporation has shown that 'US weapons and military training have 'fanned the flames of the violence in Colombia'. The report, *Arms Trafficking and Colombia*, traces the path of small arms and light weapons from US-origin stockpiles in Nicaragua, El Salvador and other Cold War battlegrounds in Central America to Colombia, where they are used by State Department-labeled terrorist groups.[26] Amnesty agrees, saying the conflict has 'driven the demand for small arms'. According to Human Rights Watch, only 25 per cent of US military assistance to Colombia is formally subject to human rights conditions.[27]

Conflict and refugees

Even a cursory glance at where most refugees and internally displaced people come from highlights the obvious connection between war, conflict and people fleeing for a better life – or even to save their lives.

The United Nations High Commissioner for Refugees (UNHCR) provides protection and assistance to refugees, internally displaced people (IDPs) and asylum seekers. At the start of 2007, the number of people of concern to UNHCR was 32.9 million, 1 in every 198 people on earth. That included 9.9 million refugees, 0.7 million asylum seekers, 0.7 million returned refugees, 12.8 million internally displaced and 1.9 million returned IDPs, plus 6.8 million others of concern.[28]

Afghans currently constitute the largest single refugee population, at around 2.1 million people. Civilians from Iraq constitute the second largest group, with 1.45 million refugees, and the Sudanese are the third largest at 686,300.

Nationalists and conservatives in the West criticize their governments for accepting refugees from abroad, and call for tighter controls and even detention of asylum seekers. It should be noted that while some Western countries are huge purveyors of arms to the regions from which refugees are fleeing, they are not unduly 'burdened' with the result of their sales. The main host countries for refugees are Pakistan, sheltering just over one million, and Iran with 968,000. The US is the main Western home to refugees, with 843,000.

1 Frida Berrigan, William D Hartung and Leslie Heffel, *US Weapons at War 2008: Beyond the Bush Legacy: Promoting Freedom or Fuelling Conflict* (New America Foundation, Dec 2008). **2** William Hartung, 'The New Business of War: Small Arms and the Proliferation of Conflict', in *Ethics and International Affairs*, Carnegie Council on Ethics and International Affairs. **3** Amnesty International, *Blood at the Crossroads: Making the case for a global Arms Trade Treaty* (ACT 30/011/2008). **4** Much of the information in this section is taken from three Amnesty International reports: *Sudan: Arming the perpetra-*

Impact on conflicts

tors of grave abuses in Darfur (AFR 54/139/2004), *Sudan: Arms continuing to fuel serious human rights violations in Darfur* (AFR 54/019/2007), and *Blood at the Crossroads: Making the case for a global Arms Trade Treaty* (ACT 30/011/2008), chapter 10. **5** *SIPRI Yearbook 2008*, chapter 2. **6** Much of the information in this section is taken from Amnesty International, *Blood at the Crossroads: Making the case for a global Arms Trade Treaty* (ACT 30/011/2008), chapter 9. **7** *Yemen Times*, 27 December 2008. **8** Foreign and Commonwealth Office, *Country Profile: Somalia*, www.fco.gov.uk **9** Roger Middleton, *Piracy in Somalia: Threatening global trade, feeding local wars*, Royal Institute of International Affairs, Oct 2008. **10** www.phrmg.org/pal_fatalities_list.htm **11** www.phrmg.org/aqsa/israeli_fatalities.htm **12** Jeremy M Sharp, *US Foreign Aid to Israel*, Congressional Research Service, 2 Jan 2008, www.fas.org/sgp/crs/mideast/RL33222.pdf. **13** See footnote 1. **14** Frida Berrigan and William D Hartung, *US Weapons at War 2008: Beyond the Bush Legacy: Promoting Freedom or Fuelling Conflict* (New America Foundation, December 2008). **15** Frida Berrigan, William D Hartung, and Leslie Heffel, *US Weapons at War 2005: Promoting Freedom or Fuelling Conflict* (World Policy Institute, Jun 2005), www.worldpolicy.org/projects/arms/reports/wawjune2005.html#14. **16** See footnote 14. **17** Much of the information in this section is taken from Amnesty International, *Fuelling conflict: Foreign arms supplies to Israel/Gaza* (MDE 15/012/2009) **18** Defence, Foreign Affairs, International Development and Trade and Industry Committees, *Strategic Export Controls: Annual Report for 2000, Licensing Policy And Prior Parliamentary Scrutiny*, House of Commons, 16 Jul 2002, HC718. **19** See footnote 18. **20** Defence, Foreign Affairs, International Development and Trade and Industry Committees, *Strategic Export Controls: Annual Report for 2001, Licensing Policy And Prior Parliamentary Scrutiny*, House of Commons, 20 May 2003, HC474). **21** Mark Curtis, *The Good, the Bad and the Ugly: A decade of Labour's arms exports*, Saferworld, May 2007. **22** Defence, Foreign Affairs, International Development and Trade and Industry Committees, *Strategic Export Controls: 2007 Review*, House of Commons, 23 July 2007, HC117. **23** Much of the information in this section is taken from Amnesty International, *Blood at the Crossroads: Making the case for a global Arms Trade Treaty*, ACT 30/011/2008,chapter 3. **24** See footnote 1. **25** Frida Berrigan and William D Hartung, *US Weapons at War 2008: Beyond the Bush Legacy: Promoting Freedom or Fuelling Conflict*, New America Foundation, December 2008. **26** Cited in Berrigan, Hartung and Heffel, see footnote 15. **27** See footnote 25. **28** *UNHCR Statistical Yearbook 2006*.

4 Impact on human rights

How weapons sales help perpetuate human rights abuses... and give political support to the countries that perpetrate them.

'No security assistance may be provided to any country the Government of which engages in a consistent pattern of gross violations of internationally recognized human rights.'
    – SECTION 502B, US FOREIGN ASSISTANCE ACT[1]

'The President shall consider the following criteria... The Government of the country... was chosen by and permits free and fair elections... respects human rights... does not persistently engage in gross violations of internationally recognized human rights, including extra-judicial or arbitrary executions, disappearances, torture or severe mistreatment, prolonged arbitrary imprisonment...'
    – US INTERNATIONAL ARMS SALES CODE OF CONDUCT ACT 1999[2]

'Having assessed the recipient country's attitude towards relevant principles established by international human rights instruments, Member states shall: deny an export license if there is a clear risk that the military technology or equipment to be exported might be used for internal repression... internal repression includes, inter alia, torture and other cruel, inhuman, and degrading treatment or punishment, summary or arbitrary executions, disappearances, arbitrary detentions and other major violations of human rights and fundamental freedoms.'
    – EU COMMON POSITION ON ARMS EXPORTS, 8 DECEMBER 2008[3]

DESPITE THE IMPRESSIVE rhetoric above, human rights have not been a major barrier to weapons sales at any time in history. The world's worst dictators, despots, human rights abusers and anti-democratic regimes have been the customers of all the major arms-producing countries in the world – and continue to be so. Campaigners have been working for years to prevent arms sales to human-rights-abusing states.

Human rights abuse takes many forms, and is not easily definable. It ranges from banning certain languages, to extra-judicial killings, from physical torture to widespread state-sponsored repression of a particular race or minority. It might include the banning of teaching of a particular philosophy, outlook or worldview. It could include an autocratic or dictatorial political system, which does not allow free elections and bans alternative political parties or visions.

Whatever the definition, the arms trade perpetuates, worsens and legitimizes the systematic abuse of human rights all over the world.

United Nations Universal Declaration of Human Rights

Article 2
Everyone is entitled to all the rights and freedoms set forth in this Declaration, without distinction of any kind, such as race, color, sex, language, religion, political or other opinion, national or social origin, property, birth or other status.

Article 5
No one shall be subjected to torture or to cruel, inhuman or degrading treatment or punishment.

Article 10
Everyone is entitled in full equality to a fair and public hearing by an independent and impartial tribunal, in the determination of his rights and obligations and of any criminal damage against him.

The full text can be viewed at www.un.org/events/humanrights/udhr60/declaration.shtml

The supply of equipment that can be used to carry out human rights abuses, such as small arms, military vehicles and other hardware, supports the abuse because it provides oppressors with the tools to carry out their actions. And those actions need not be directly connected to the equipment in question. A military vehicle that carries soldiers to burn down a refugee camp is as involved in the abuse as the weapons and soldiers themselves. Even if an imported military vehicle is not used to carry soldiers to the refugee camp, it increases the capacity of the military.

In addition, arms sales always carry with them a political value. Whatever arms are being supplied to a regime, whether or not they are used in human rights abuses, they confer political and moral legitimacy to the state to which they are being sold. Whether Hawk aircraft, supplied by Britain to Indonesia, were used over East Timor or not is irrelevant in the sense that their sale helped to confer legitimacy upon the murderous Suharto regime.

Western democracies like to argue that they use arms sales as bargaining chips in negotiations with countries with repressive human rights records, in order to urge them to clean up their act. But there is little evidence to suggest this.

The following four case studies demonstrate the negative impact of the arms trade on human rights. The cases are varied, as are the suppliers.

Nepal[4]

Nepal was until 2006 ruled by a monarchy. In 1990, following widespread demands for democracy, a virtually bloodless revolution produced a parliamentary system of government. In 1996 the Communist Party of Nepal (Maoist) – CPN(M) – launched a 'people's war'.

In 2001, a royal massacre, in which the King and Queen were killed, resulted in the indefinite postponement of elections. In 2005 a state of emergency was imposed by the King in which many fundamental human rights were suspended and strict media censorship introduced. Widespread human rights violations were reported.

Between 1996 and 2005, over 12,000 people were killed in the 'people's war', many at the hands of the Royal Nepal Army (RNA). Amnesty reported: 'throughout the conflict, a consistent failure to hold members of the security forces accountable for their actions and a lack of transparency has created a culture of impunity and increased the vulnerability of the civilian population'. The CPN(M) were responsible for widespread killings of civilians, abductions, and torture, as well as the use of child soldiers.

India, traditionally the main source of supply for the RNA, has supplied, among other things, rifles, helicopter gunships, jeeps, trucks, and ammunition, as well as military training.

Between 2000 and 2004 the British Government gifted a wide range of 'non-lethal' equipment to Nepal, including trucks, Land Rovers, helicopters and surveillance equipment. Like India, Britain has provided extensive training to the RNA.

Since 2001, the US has provided $29 million in military grants to Nepal, including 20,000 assault rifles and training. In 2004 the US Congress passed a law requiring Nepal to improve its human rights record if it wanted to continue receiving assistance.

Western countries have also permitted private arms sales to Nepal, despite concerns over the human rights situation. The British Government in 2001 granted £6 million ($9 million) worth of export licenses, including for 6,780 assault rifles, as well as weapons sights and grenade launchers. In 2002 Belgium permitted the export of 3,000 FN Herstal light machine guns to Nepal. In 2003 South Africa permitted the export of military communication equipment.

Amnesty has documented how the RNA used its

helicopters to, in some instances, deliberately target civilians. Amnesty has also documented examples of human rights violations committed by the RNA with small arms.

In the late 1990s, the Nepalese Government's conduct in the war largely escaped international criticism. After the 11 September 2001 attacks on the US, the Nepalese Government presented its campaign against the CPN(M) as a fight against 'terrorism' to win military assistance from the West.

Violent clashes occurred between protesters and security forces in 2006, with the Nepalese security forces widely condemned by the international community. The unrest eventually resulted in the abdication of the King and the CPN(M) leading a coalition government.

Indonesia[5]

Indonesia is a classic example of a country with a repressive military armed by Western powers anxious to maintain Indonesia's friendship for geopolitical reasons.

In October 1965, a botched coup against President Sukarno resulted in General Suharto taking power. Suharto initiated a six-month orgy of killing against the Indonesian Communist Party (PKI), described by Amnesty as ranking 'among the most massive violations of human rights since the Second World War'. The killings took the lives of at least half a million Indonesians. Suharto then set up a military dictatorship, ruling Indonesia until 1998.

Britain and the US welcomed the Suharto takeover and gave him considerable support throughout his time in power. In 1975, Indonesia invaded East Timor and occupied it, at the cost eventually of up to 183,000 lives. Despite this, British Aerospace sold Indonesia Hawk ground-attack aircraft in 1978, 1981, 1982 and 1983.

Impact on human rights

Despite the Indonesian Army's massacre of over 400 civilians at a peaceful demonstration in Dili, East Timor, in 1991, Britain permitted more major arms deals with Indonesia. In 1993 and 1996 Indonesia bought more Hawk aircraft from British Aerospace, and in 1995 and 1996 Scorpion tanks and Stormer armored vehicles from Alvis.

General Suharto was forced to stand down in 1998, following the Asian economic crisis of the late 1990s. He was never punished for his crimes, and lived his twilight years in luxurious retirement until his death in 2008.

The vicious occupation of East Timor only came to an end in 1999, after the people of East Timor (now Timor-Leste) voted overwhelmingly for independence from Indonesia. They did so despite an Indonesian-backed campaign of terror, which cost around 1,500 lives and devastated the country. This occurred despite

---

Examples of Indonesian Army use of British-supplied equipment in internal repression

• In April 1996, British-supplied armored personnel carriers were used in a violent assault on the campus of the Islamic University of Indonesia in Ujung Pandang. The British Government acknowledged that British equipment supplied in the 1960s was used in this attack and that excessive force was used to repress legitimate protest;

• Throughout 1998, British-supplied Scorpions, armored vehicles and water cannon were regularly photographed and filmed on the streets of Indonesian cities putting down peaceful protests against the rule of President Suharto and his successor, President Habibie. British-supplied equipment was used on 12 May when four students were killed at Trisakti University, Jakarta, and on 13 November when more than a dozen people were killed in Jakarta. The British Foreign Secretary acknowledged that some of the equipment being used against demonstrators was sold by Britain;

• In July and December 2000, British-supplied Saladins were used in Ambon in clashes between Christians and Muslims;

• In 2003 and 2004 British-supplied Scorpion tanks were on several occasions filmed attacking separatist positions in Aceh. ■

Indonesia having promised the UN it would maintain peace and security throughout.

Although Suharto's ousting and East Timor's independence were positive developments, the human rights situation in Indonesia remained poor through the early years of this century.

In 1976 an armed separatist movement had become active in the Indonesian province of Aceh. Indonesian military operations were stepped up in 1989. In the 1990s, thousands of civilians were killed, mostly by the Indonesian Army as it attempted to crush the separatists. After Suharto's fall from power, the level of violence increased year-on-year up to the end of 2002, when a tentative peace agreement was reached. However, in May 2003 the agreement broke down and the Indonesian Government launched a major military operation in the province. Many atrocities were committed against Acehnese civilians.

Prior to August 2002, the Indonesian Government had agreed not to use British-supplied equipment in Aceh, and to inform the British Government in advance if it planned to do so. However, in August 2002, the British Government, at Indonesia's request, allowed the use of British-supplied equipment in Aceh by the Indonesian Army.

This decision in effect gave a green light for war crimes to the Indonesian Army. At the same time, during 2002, the British Government tripled the number of licenses issued for arms to Indonesia (up to 182 from 54 in 2001). Subsequently, British-supplied Scorpion tanks, Hawk aircraft and Saracen armored personnel carriers joined the war in Aceh in 2003.

The British Government said they had assurances from Indonesia that the weapons would not be used 'offensively' or 'in breach of human rights'. Given the Indonesian 'assurances' to the UN had meant nothing in East Timor, and the examples of previous use of British-supplied equipment in internal repression, this was an astonishing position to adopt.

A Parliamentary Committee discovered the British Government took no independent action to check how the Indonesian Army was using British equipment. It concluded that the 'assurances are not worth the paper they are written on'. In 2005 the Government was forced to abandon the use of such assurances.

No thanks to Britain, the war in Aceh had by then come to an end. The tsunami on Boxing Day 2004 devastated Aceh, and prompted the start of a negotiated peace process which finally brought an end to the terrible war in the province.

Guinea[6]

Guinea, in West Africa, a French colony from the late 19th century onwards, gained independence in 1958. The first President, Sekou Touré, was an autocrat and suppressed opposition. General Lasana Conté, who took over in a bloodless coup in 1984 after Touré's death, died at the end of 2008. Conté reverted to the oppressive methods of the Touré years after an attempted coup in 1985.

In 1991 Conté was forced by public pressure to introduce elections. A regular feature of the elections held since then, which Conté won, has been disputes about their validity and opposition complaints of harassment by the security forces.

Guinea's human rights record has been poor since independence. The security forces in Guinea violently suppressed demonstrations during the December 1998 presidential elections, the local elections of June 2000, and the 2001 referendum on Conté's self-serving proposal to scrap the two-term limit on presidential office.

Hence Amnesty said there was a 'foreseeable and significant risk' that the Guinea security forces would use military equipment in serious human rights violations. Nevertheless, in 2003, South Africa allowed

Alvis OMC, the South African subsidiary of a British company, Alvis, to supply Mamba armored vehicles to Guinea.

In January and February 2007 there were mainly peaceful demonstrations in Guinea protesting against corruption and judicial interference by Conté. Film footage shot on 22 January in the capital, Conakry, showed security forces in what appeared to be Mamba and other vehicles, firing on demonstrators at a peaceful rally. The use of force by the security forces over the two months left more than 130 dead and 1,500 injured. Children were also fired on by the security forces. A law was passed to set up a Commission of Inquiry into the violations, but was starved of funds by the Government and could not start work.

Since 2003, when the potential for violence by the security forces against peaceful protesters was self-evident, France, Portugal and Spain have all supplied shotgun cartridges to the regime, Senegal has delivered munitions and Turkey firearms.

These exports were made despite the persistent pattern of human rights abuses by the security forces in Guinea. They are a good example of how arms-producing nations assist in perpetuating political repression in the developing world.

Burma[7]
Burma, often known as Myanmar, was from 1885 part of British colonial India, becoming independent in 1948. In March 1962 a Burmese General staged a coup and the country was subsequently run by a 'Revolutionary Council' of generals which resulted in economic stagnation and isolation.

In 1988 the regime was challenged by popular protest, demanding elected civilian government. In September, the State Law and Order Council (SLORC) took power and killed thousands of demonstrators in a brutal crackdown.

Impact on human rights

In the run-up to elections in 1990, Aung San Suu Kyi, the leader of the most popular opposition party, was placed under house arrest, where she remains. Although the opposition overwhelmingly won the 1990 elections, they were annulled by the SLORC. The regime is implementing a 'road map' to democracy, though this is not considered a credible or inclusive process by most observers.

The Burmese security forces have a well-documented history of serious human rights abuses, which the UN has described as widespread and systematic.

In 1988, the EU placed an arms embargo on Burma, with the US following in 1993. However, since 1988, China has been the main supplier of arms to the Burmese military. It has supplied tanks, armored personnel carriers, military aircraft and artillery. In 2002 China told the UN it had delivered 3,200 firearms to Burma.

Other countries that have supplied Burma include Russia, Serbia and the Ukraine. Russia has supplied artillery and combat aircraft, Serbia has supplied artillery systems and the Ukraine has supplied armored personnel carriers. Ten years ago, reports indicate, Singapore supplied Burma with a factory to produce assault rifles and ammunition. Other reports suggest India has offered to sell a variety of military equipment to Burma, although India has reassured the EU it will not sell helicopters to Burma containing components made in Europe.

In September 2007 protests became widespread due to the Burmese Government dramatically increasing the price of fuel, resulting in the largest display of civil unrest in Burma since 1988.

The protests, led by monks, quickly spread. They were suppressed with live ammunition, tear gas and batons. Thousands were arrested (hundreds held in conditions that amounted to inhumane treatment with credible reports of torture), hundreds injured and at least 31 killed.

The Burmese Army used military trucks supplied by a Chinese company to carry troops during the repression. Between 1988 and 1995 China provided about 1,000 vehicles to Burma, and a Chinese company reportedly sold 400 in 2005. Military trucks drove into a crowd and killed at least three people in the capital, Yangon, in September 2007.

China and Russia, two permanent members of the UN Security Council, blocked an attempt to impose a UN arms embargo on Burma. This diplomatic backing provides the Burmese Government with no reason to improve its behavior, as it knows it has friends from whom it can buy the military equipment it needs to repress democratic forces in Burma.

1 http://tinyurl.com/mmva5 2 http://tinyurl.com/d9mopy 3 http://tinyurl.com/bnk68u 4 Much of the information in this section is taken from Amnesty International, Nepal: Military assistance contributing to grave human rights violations (ASA 31/047/2005). 5 Much of the information in this section is taken from Campaign Against Arms Trade, www.caat.org.uk/publications/countries/indonesia-0604.php 6 Much of the information in this section is taken from Amnesty International, Blood at the Crossroads: Making the case for a global Arms Trade Treaty (ACT 30/011/2008), chapter 6. 7 Much of the information in this section is taken from Amnesty International, Blood at the Crossroads: Making the case for a global Arms Trade Treaty (ACT 30/011/2008), chapter 8.

5 Impact on development

Debt as the legacy of military borrowing... Effect of conflict on development and the Millennium Development Goals... Development and arms-trade related corruption... Steps being taken to attempt to halt the arms trade affecting development.

'IT IS NOT possible for the community of nations to achieve any of its major goals – not peace, not environmental protection, not human rights or democratization, not fertility reduction nor social integration – except in the context of sustainable development that leads to human security.' These words, which appeared in the UN Human Development Report in 1994, still hold true today.

Sustainable development is greatly threatened by conflict. As former World Bank economist Paul Collier has written, 'developing countries have enough problems without either the waste of resources constituted by military expenditure, or the social and economic destruction brought about by warfare'.[1]

Despite improvements over the past few decades, there are still an estimated 1.4 billion people who live in deepest poverty (defined by the World Bank as living on less than $1.25 per day at 2005 prices). According to the World Bank: 'in Sub-Saharan Africa, the $1.25 a day poverty rate has shown no sustained decline over the whole period since 1981, starting and ending at around 50 per cent. In absolute terms, the number of poor people has nearly doubled, from 200 million in 1981 to 380 million in 2005.'[2]

The Cold War legacy
The poorest countries in the world are so poor largely because of huge debts owed to the developed world, some of it repayments for past arms sales. Many of the most heavily indebted countries are currently engaged

in, or emerging from, conflict of some kind.

Arms sales fuel a never-ending vicious cycle of poverty and debt. During the Cold War, developing nations found themselves filing in behind one or the other of the major world powers, buying or receiving free arms to strengthen their position. This in turn fueled local arms races.

At the same time, dictators and corrupt governments were making large-scale arms purchases, both to bolster their own power and to line their pockets with generous kickbacks and bribes from each sale. High military spending reduced outlay on development and increased the occurrence of cross-border and internal conflicts. This created a need for more arms, which were bought using Western loans, thereby adding to the country's debt.

Post-Cold War, the cycle continues in many parts of Africa and Asia. In some regions, nations are suffering the economic effects of decades of borrowing, crushed under the weight of debts that do not really belong to them, which they have no hope of ever paying off.

At the height of the Cold War in the 1970s and 1980s, the world's poorest regions were caught up in an arms race that is, arguably, the foundation for their poverty today. Central America, the Horn of Africa, southern Africa and Indo-China were drawn into the tensions, which exacerbated regional arms races and localized conflicts. In 1985, Mozambique allocated 38 per cent of government spending to the military, Iran spent 34.1 per cent, El Salvador 29.1 per cent, Ethiopia 28.9 per cent and Nicaragua 26.2 per cent. In most cases, arms purchases meant military expenditure had to be increased and budgets for development were tightened. In other cases, the countries borrowed hard currency from international lenders to fund their arms purchases, or simply went into debt to the arms-supplying nation.

According to a report by the Campaign Against

Impact on development

Arms Trade (CAAT): 'The debts and costs of destruction that accumulated during the Cold War will remain a burden for generations to come. Children not yet born will have to pay the price of debt for wars they did not fight, for ideas they do not hold, for a regional and global system that no longer exists and for decisions made by regional and world leaders no longer in power.'[3] A research paper written in 1994 estimated that a fifth of all developing-world debt was due to arms purchases.[4]

The Millennium Development Goals and conflict

At the beginning of the century, 189 countries got together and agreed to set themselves eight Millennium Development Goals (MDG). These were to aim by 2015 to:
- Halve extreme poverty and hunger
- Achieve universal primary education
- Promote gender equality and empower women
- Reduce child mortality
- Improve maternal health
- Combat HIV/AIDS, malaria, and other diseases
- Ensure environmental sustainability
- Develop a global partnership for development

Developing countries are particularly prone to experiencing armed conflict. As War on Want has noted, '80 per cent of the world's 20 poorest countries have suffered a major war in the past 15 years'.[5] Collier argues that 'countries with low per capita income, slow or negative growth, and dependence upon primary commodity exports [in other words, developing countries], are considerably more at risk than other countries'. Hence the arms trade, by providing the weapons used in these conflicts, has a particularly adverse effect on development and the likelihood of achieving the MDGs.

This state of affairs looks unlikely to improve soon. As we saw in Chapter 1, most wars these days are civil wars rather than wars between countries. Collier notes that 'for developing countries by far the most common form of war is civil war'. During such wars, according to Collier, the economic growth rate of a country is typically reduced by around two per cent. He cites recent analysis showing that civil wars are getting longer – and now continue for around three times as long as wars which happened prior to 1980.

Effect of conflict on development

Developing countries suffer accordingly. For example War on Want has noted that 9 of the 10 countries with the world's highest child mortality rates have suffered from conflict in recent years. Oxfam says 'both adult and infant mortality rates increase by 13 per cent during armed conflict. Maternal mortality rates, and the prevalence of illnesses such as HIV and AIDS, all increase too'.[6]

Oxfam has reported that at least 22 of the 34 countries least likely to achieve the MDGs are either in the middle of conflict or recently emerging from it. Sub-Saharan Africa, a region prone to conflict, likely will not meet any of the MDGs by 2015.

Let's look closer at a few countries. In the Democratic Republic of the Congo (DRC), 4.8 million died over the period 1998 to 2006, during and after the conflict there. According to Oxfam, 90 per cent of these deaths were due to preventable infectious diseases, malnutrition and pregnancy-related conditions. It is difficult to believe that this would have happened in a country at peace, even one as poor as the DRC. For the war in the DRC cost the country an estimated $18 billion, but in 2006, the Gross Domestic Product of the DRC was estimated by the International Monetary Fund at just under $17.5 billion.[7] According to Control Arms around half the weapons used in the war in the DRC were Kalashnikov assault rifles or similar.[8] Kalashnikovs are not produced in the DRC.

Impact on development

In Burundi, which borders the DRC, around 300,000 were killed and a million forced to flee their homes in a civil war that lasted from 1993 to 2006. The estimated cost of this war has been put at $5.7 billion.[9] According to Oxfam, Burundi's health statistics are shocking and 'a significant factor has been the virtual destruction of health services during the war, and the continuing armed violence is a significant drain on what little healthcare infrastructure remains'. They note Burundi's lack of an arms industry; therefore all the weapons used to fight this conflict were imported from other countries.

In Liberia the various conflicts which took place between 1989 and 2003 resulted in 250,000 deaths and around 1 million being displaced.[10] Despite UN arms embargoes Liberia's wars were fueled by imports of arms from Asia and Europe, often via the Middle East and other African countries. Liberia's health statistics are also appalling, but the reduction in violence has now enabled significant increases in school enrollment rates.

In Sudan, a recent report notes, 'the enormous mineral wealth of Sudan is being diverted from development into an arms race' with the Government spending 40 per cent of its money on the military and public order in 2006, with the autonomous Government of Southern Sudan spending 30 per cent in 2008. But the changed atmosphere since the peace agreement in Southern Sudan shows how wasteful this is. People can move around the area freely, there are adequate pharmaceutical supplies for the first time, primary enrollment has increased dramatically, and most of the displaced population have returned.[11]

These and other conflicts in Africa, fought largely with weapons from abroad, have taken a heavy economic toll. Oxfam estimates that between 1990 and 2005, 23 African countries lost around $284 billion because of armed conflict. In those conflicts

95 per cent of the arms and ammunition came from abroad.

Development and arms-trade related debt and corruption
Development can also be adversely affected by spending on the arms trade that does not result in conflict. Even in countries not embroiled in significant armed conflict, excessive military spending, debt and corruption caused by arms purchases can make it harder for development goals to be achieved.

For example, some countries classified by the UN as having 'low human development' spend more on the military than on education and health combined (Eritrea, Angola, Burundi and the DRC) while others spend more on the military than on health (Guinea, Côte d'Ivoire, Guinea-Bissau).[12]

Turkey, a NATO member, has for many years been a major arms importer. By 1999, between 10 to 20 per cent of its debt was related to arms purchases made since 1990. Turkey has continued to spend on weapons in this century too. Turkey's arms-related debt has increased by at least $10 billion between 2000 and 2007, according to SIPRI. The country's 2005 MDG report says that Turkey's debt has led to cutbacks which 'impact negatively on the allocation of funds for any policies targeting improvements of social welfare in general... and poverty alleviation in particular'.[13]

Corruption is a significant problem too. In India, another major arms importer, 47 arms deals were under police corruption investigation in 2005. Senior politicians and officers have been accused of taking bribes, and some deals with implicated companies have been canceled. India will be unlikely to meet any of the MDGs unless it changes its spending priorities away from the military.[14]

In South Africa, a massive arms deal which has already led to convictions for corruption (see chapter

Impact on development

7) is costing an average of $530 million a year until 2011/12, when $425 million a year would pay for free water services for the whole country.[15]

What is being done about this?

A progressive attitude towards helping developing countries emerge from the cycle of debt and conflict depends on a two-handed approach.

First, Western nations must write off the huge debts owed to them by the very poorest nations. Take Indonesia. This is a poor country which suffered greatly in the Asian financial crisis of 1998. It has the highest maternal mortality rate in Southeast Asia[16] and has 14 million (6 per cent of the population) living on less than $1 per day and 117 million (54 per cent) living on less than $2 per day.[17]

During the 1990s Indonesia spent lavishly on Hawk aircraft from BAe and armored vehicles from Alvis (a deal about which corruption allegations subsequently emerged). These deals were guaranteed by Britain's Export Credits Guarantee Department (ECGD). In the 1998 crisis Indonesia defaulted on its debts, so ECGD paid the arms companies the guarantee it had given, leaving the British Government to recover the money from Indonesia.

Between 1998 and 2004 ECGD paid £645 million ($965 million) to British arms companies because of the Indonesian default.[18] At the end of February 2007, ECGD had £757 million of claims outstanding for Indonesia. About three-quarters of these related to arms sales, with 60 per cent accounted for by the sale of Hawk aircraft in the 1990s.[19]

Although Indonesia is a poor country, the British Government continues to insist Indonesia pays debts incurred for previous arms purchases. The debt will be paid off in 2021. Although this will mean the British taxpayer will not lose money (assuming all goes to plan), the arms trade will have inflicted a cruel financial burden on Indonesia.

Second, Western nations should cease selling arms to the very poorest countries, thereby preventing new debts from accumulating and helping at least to stem the flow of weapons. The EU Code of Conduct on Arms Sales (see chapter 9), which was finally introduced in 1998 after many years of lobbying by campaigners, urged arms-selling European states to consider 'whether the proposed export would seriously hamper the sustainable development of the recipient country' when granting arms export licenses. The new EU Common Position essentially leaves this unchanged.

But the EU Code and Common Position have had little effect, so far, in preventing arms exports to some of the poorest and most underdeveloped nations. A recent British Parliamentary enquiry was 'surprised to learn that since 2002 only one application to export arms had been refused by the British Government on the grounds that it was incompatible with the technical and economic capacity of the recipient country'. The British Government defended itself against the criticisms of campaigners by saying 'exports to developing countries make up a relatively small proportion of the global trade in military equipment, and of the UK's military exports'. Other EU countries have done little better – only 52 export licenses (out of tens of thousands issued) have been refused because of sustainable development concerns since 2003, and 42 of those have been refused by one country – France.[20] Sweden does not even have a methodology for assessing whether an arms deal would threaten sustainable development.[21]

The US Congressional Research service says, however, that 'developing countries continue to be the primary focus of foreign arms sales activity by weapons suppliers'.[22] The value of arms deals with developing nations increased in 2007 to $42.3 billion from $38.1 billion a year before. The US and Russia dominate the arms market in the developing world. Looking at Africa, between 2000 and 2007, China, and European countries (with the exception of Britain, France, Germany and Italy) were the top two deal makers with Africa.[23]

The arms trade's effect on conflict, human rights and development, then, is overwhelmingly negative. But how is the 'business of death' actually conducted?

1 Paul Collier, 'War and military expenditure in developing countries and their consequences for development' in *The Economics of Peace and Security Journal*, vol 1, no 1, 2006. **2** http://tinyurl.com/d56gsu **3** Susan Willett, *The arms trade, debt and development*, Campaign Against Arms Trade, May 1999. **4** *Shooting Down the MDGs: How irresponsible arms transfers undermine development goals*, Oxfam, Oct 2008. **5** Fabien Mathieu and Nick Dearden, *Corporate Mercenaries: The threat of private military and security companies*, War on Want, Nov 2006. **6** See footnote 4. **7** http://tinyurl.com/bol37w **8** *The AK-47: the world's favourite killing machine*, Control Arms, Jun 2006. **9** See footnote 4. **10** See footnote 9. **11** Edward Thomas, *Against the Gathering Storm: Securing Sudan's Comprehensive Peace Agreement*, Royal Institute of International Affairs, Jan 2009. **12** http://hdr.undp.org/en/reports/global/hdr2007-2008/ **13** See footnote 4. **14** See footnote 4. **15** See footnote 4. **16** See footnote 4. **17** www.dfid.gov.uk/countries/asia/indonesia.asp **18** Hansard, 18 Nov 2004. **19** Hansard, 12 Mar 2007. **20** Defence, Foreign Affairs, International Development and Trade and Industry Committees, *Strategic Export Controls: 2007 Review*, House of Commons, 23 Jul 2007, HC117. **21** *Good conduct? Ten years of the EU Code of Conduct on Arms Exports*, Jun 2008. **22** Congressional Research Service, *Conventional Arms Transfers to Developing Nations, 2000-2007*, 23 Oct 2007. **23** See footnote 22.

6 The business of death

The 'revolving door' and peddling political influence... Arms fairs and DSEi... Government subsidies and other financial support... The jobs arguments... Mercenaries... Espionage.

THE ARMS COMPANIES like to say that arms companies and government are completely separate, with the corporations at the mercy of legislators. This is far from the truth. Not only do weapons manufacturers wield political influence with their constant threats of job losses, but in some countries they also make financial contributions to political parties in the hope of commanding influence.

The distinction is further blurred by what has become known as the 'revolving door' – simply put, government ministers, advisers and senior members of the armed forces frequently move into the employment of arms companies and vice versa. The supposed wall between government and the industry has a huge gaping hole in it, in which a constantly revolving door has been established.

Let's look first at people working in government who move into the arms industry.[1] The Advisory Committee on Business Appointments in Britain approves senior members of the Government moving into private employment. In 2004 it reported: 'in the case of the [Ministry of Defence] it can be argued that the numbers seeking such employment are so significant as to amount to a "traffic" from the Department to the defense contractors who supply it'. A similar 'revolving door' operates in the US, where a recent Government Accountability Office study showed that in 2006, 2,435 former Pentagon officers and officials worked in the arms industry.[2]

This applies to politicians as well as officials and

soldiers. Since the start of the 1990s at least nine British Defence Ministers have gained jobs with arms companies. Senior military officers, including former Chiefs of the Defence Staff, senior Ministry of Defence (MoD) procurement officials, and former advisers to the Prime Minister have also gone into the arms industry since 1997.

Throughout its 41-year history the British Government's Defence Export Services Organization (DESO) drew its heads from the arms industry. Other arms industry employees are regularly seconded into government.

The arms industry is also over-represented on British Government 'advisory bodies'. Of the 19 military-related advisory bodies where Campaign Against Arms Trade (CAAT) had membership information in 2005, BAES had a representative on 17, Rolls Royce on 15, and the Society of British Aerospace Companies on 13. The four main bodies had 81 members – 45 from industry, 28 from Government and only eight from elsewhere. Individuals and companies linked to arms companies have also been donors or sponsors to the governing Labour Party.

The problem of arms fairs

Fairs and exhibitions are the most outward manifestation of the tendency of the arms trade to supply countries currently at war or in conflict with each other. Every year countries shop at exhibitions taking place all over the world. Arms companies show their very best weaponry – their most modern killing and 'defense' equipment. Arms fairs are the hub of the international arms trade.

The deals do take place at the fairs themselves, but these are also meeting and networking places – where delegates can begin relationships with the companies, later going on to discuss, in private, their military needs and what is available.

Countries hosting arms fairs often argue that they would not necessarily sell *matériel* to every country that attends, but this is a bluff. Every delegate invited to an arms fair is a potential customer, not just for the host nation, but for every corporate exhibitor.

Most arms fairs happen biennially, and there are at least 30 major arms fairs as well as numerous minor ones. They range from 'tri-service' arms fairs (which exhibit arms and equipment for land, sea and air armed forces), to aerospace exhibitions, naval exhibitions and other specialist fairs.

Some major arms fairs[3]

Africa Aero and Defence
This biennial exhibition takes place in South Africa and covers a range of aerospace and military exhibits. South African General Julius Kriel has said it is 'very much a show for Africa'.

Defendory
This biennial exhibition takes place in Greece, and was originally set up in 1980 to ensure Greece had access to arms imports. Now it has been described as one of the world's premier military exhibitions.

Eurosatory
This biennial arms fair in Paris describes itself as an international exhibition for land and land-air defense. It is probably the biggest dedicated military land show in Europe. Paris also hosts the largest air show in the world.

IDEAS Pakistan
This biennial show is organized on behalf of the Pakistani Government. It focuses on weapons, military vehicles and most other military equipment. Since Pakistan has explicitly said it would probably only rule out Israel as a customer, IDEAS can cater to the military needs of various pariah states. Previous state attendees include North Korea, Burma, and Zimbabwe.

IDEX
IDEX is the largest arms fair in the Middle East, and is held biennially in Abu Dhabi in the United Arab Emirates.

Latin America Aero and Defense
This fair is the main Latin American arms fair, held biennially in Brazil. It exhibits military products for air, sea and land, as well as civilian aircraft.

The business of death

Aerospace exhibitions typically cover both military and civilian aircraft, as it is good PR for the arms companies to incorporate 'public days' and aerobatic shows into the event. As CAAT has noted, specialist shows include naval fairs such as Gulf Maritime in the United Arab Emirates, EuroNaval in Paris and ExpoNaval in Chile. Other niche areas include 'internal security' (for example Milipol Paris), special forces (for example SOFEX in Jordan), helicopters (for example Helitech at Duxford, near Cambridge in Britain). There have also been small specialist shows relating to pilotless aerial vehicles.

Flagship fair

DSEi – Defence Systems Equipment International – since 1999 has been Britain's flagship arms fair, replacing the lumbering Royal Navy and British Army Equipment Exhibition with a sparkling new, slick-running private show. Since 2001 DSEi has taken place at the ExCel exhibition center in London's Docklands, and is booked to return in 2011.

It has been mired in controversy from the beginning. In 1999, there were two separate breaches of brand new British legislation banning the manufacture and sale of anti-personnel landmines.

After privatization in 1997, DSEi was owned by Spearhead, a private company that was then part of the US corporation PGI. The day before DSEi 2003, Spearhead was acquired by global publishing giant Reed Elsevier. DSEi has enjoyed British Government backing, with senior ministers regularly attending and demonstrations of equipment made by the British armed forces. Human-rights-abusing states are invited as a matter of routine: 2007's included China, Libya, Colombia and Saudi Arabia.

Campaigners have scored a notable victory by forcing Reed Elsevier to give up its involvement with DSEi, a blow to those trying to portray arms fairs as a legitimate business area. The campaign, launched in 2005, included an open letter in *The Lancet* signed by senior doctors and healthcare experts. This prompted *The Lancet*'s editorial board to call on Reed Elsevier 'to divest itself of all business interests that threaten human, and especially civilian, health and well-being'. The *British Medical Journal* took up the call too.

In March 2006, 13 internationally renowned writers, including AS Byatt, Ian McEwan and JM Coetzee, called upon Reed Elsevier, organizers of the London Book Fair, to end their involvement in the global arms trade. Nearly 2,000 academics signed a petition in August 2006, followed in March 2007 by an open letter to the *Times Higher Education Supplement*, where 138 academics from 17 countries demanded Reed Elsevier cease all involvement in arms fairs.

In June 2007 Reed Elsevier announced it would sell its international arms fair business. The Chief Executive of Reed Elsevier, Sir Crispin Davis, said: 'It has become increasingly clear that growing numbers of important customers and authors have very real concerns about our involvement in the defense exhibitions business. We have listened closely to these concerns and this has led us to conclude that the defense shows are no longer compatible with Reed Elsevier's position as a leading publisher of scientific, medical, legal and business content.'

Reed Elsevier did not renew its contract to organize Taiwan's TADTE arms fair, sold IDEX, and in May 2007 announced it had sold its three remaining arms fairs, including London's DSEi arms fair, to Clarion Events.

Like Reed, Clarion Events focuses mainly on non-military businesses. Owned by US private equity group Veronis Suhler Stevenson, it has not previously run arms fairs; it organizes around 80 exhibitions across Britain, Europe, North America, Africa and

Arms Fair

The following shows the countries invited to attend DSEi 2007 by the British Government.

- * 'countries of concern' in the British Government's Human Rights Annual Report 2007
- † countries where armed conflict was taking place in 2007

Algeria†	Hungary	Philippines†
Australia	India†	Poland
Austria	Indonesia	Portugal
Bahrain	Iraq*	Qatar
Botswana	Ireland	Romania
Brazil	Italy	Russia*†
Brunei	Japan	Saudi Arabia*
Bulgaria	Jordan	Singapore
Canada	Kuwait	Slovakia
Chile	Libya	South Africa
China*	Malaysia	South Korea
Colombia*†	Mexico	Spain
Croatia	Morocco	Sweden
Czech Republic	Netherlands	Switzerland
Denmark	New Zealand	Trinidad & Tobago
Estonia	Norway	Turkey†
Finland	Oman	UAE
France	Pakistan*†	USA
Germany	Peru	Vietnam*
Greece		

Asia. Its shows include The Baby Show, the Spirit of Christmas Fair, the Luxury Travel Fair, Antiques for Everyone and Music Live.

Dubious practices at DSEi

Despite a huge number of controversial sales, allegations of dirty deals and illegal behavior at arms fairs all over the world, the fairs still receive only cursory monitoring from Western governments, and no monitoring at all when they take place in the Middle East and in the developing world.

Thank goodness then for investigative journalists who consistently reveal dubious practices at arms fairs. They supply arms campaigners with ample material to challenge governments to tighten up legislation on arms sales, and improve checks for potentially illegal deals.

Activist and comedian Mark Thomas attended DSEi in 2005 and told a committee of MPs in the British Parliament that he had seen TAR Ideal Concepts Ltd, an Israeli company, and Global Armour, a South African company, offering electro shock weapons. Imperial Armour, another South African company, he said, offered stun weapons and started negotiating a deal from the fair. When the evidence came to light two stalls were closed down.

The Committee reported its dismay that 'a journalist was able to identify with apparently little effort *prima facie* evidence of breaches of export control at DSEi in 2005 while HMRC [the British Customs authorities], who attended the fair, did not notice the possible potential breaches in the brochures'. It recommended the British Government 'actively seeks out breaches of export controls at arms fairs'.[4]

The extent of government subsidies

Governments subsidize their arms sector in a number of ways. The difficult job for campaigners and academics is to show by how much, and why it is a bad thing.

Strong, well-informed estimates based on obtainable information are usually the best that campaigners can muster before issuing the challenge to governments: if we are wrong, it falls to you to prove how wrong. After all, if arms exports *are* big earners for state economies, wouldn't politicians be shouting it from the roof tops?

With that proviso in mind, valiant attempts to look at this issue have been made.

In Britain, a 2004 study *Escaping the Subsidy Trap* by researchers at the British American Security Information Council (BASIC), the Oxford Research

Group, and Saferworld calculated 'that total subsidies to arms exports are at least £453 million [$680 million]*, and possibly up to £936 million'.[5]

'We estimate that the subsidies provided to UK companies involved in defense exports are worth… between £7,000 and £14,400 [$21,600] for each job supported by exports,' the report noted. British economist and journalist Samuel Brittan has argued convincingly that there is an 'inflated view of the role of arms and export promotion in the British economy'.[6]

This study is almost five years old. However, CAAT currently estimates the subsidies still total at least £500 million ($750 million) per year.

Direct subsidies – Governments' direct financial support for their arms exports can be roughly placed

---

Lending a helping hand

A breakdown of how Britain subsidizes its arms export business, in £m

Net subsidy	£m
Defence Export Services Organization	14
Defence Attachés	6
Use of armed forces for promotion	6
Defence Assistance Fund	5
Export credits	222
Ministry of Defence procurement distortion	200
Total	**453 ($680)**
Support for development of systems	up to 483
Grand total	up to 936

Paul Ingram and Roy Isbister, *Escaping the Subsidy Trap: Why arms exports are bad for Britain* (BASIC, Oxford Research Group and Saferworld, September 2004).

---

* Where sterling amounts have been converted into dollars it has been at a notional exchange rate of £1=$1.5. The exchange rate fluctuates so much that the dollar figures are only given as ballpark estimates for the convenience of the reader; they do not relate to exchange rate values at the time of the transaction.

into a few distinct categories. Each of these subsidies results in taxpayers' money being spent, or risked, helping foreign governments to buy arms.

Export promotion – The major arms-exporting countries each year spend huge amounts of money all over the world promoting and marketing their domestic arms companies' products. Export promotion includes diplomatic visits by politicians. For example, during 2001 and 2002, when India and Pakistan had mobilized their armies for war, the British Prime Minister Tony Blair and other ministers made 17 visits to the region. On many of these visits they promoted arms sales. Export promotion also includes the provision of advice and support for companies marketing their systems.

Britain has a specific government organization for promoting arms exports. It is the Defence and Security Organization, part of UK Trade and Investment (called the Defence Export Services Organization or DESO until April 2008). In 2008/9, it had an operating budget of £11.7 million ($17.5 million).[7] Its own analysis of staffing levels leads CAAT to conclude that arms selling has staff numbers comparable to every other UK Trade and Investment sector put together.

Export credits – Government insurance schemes to compensate arms companies when their foreign clients default on payment generally make up the bulk of the government direct subsidies. They also provide financing support for deals. Governments then attempt to recoup the cost from the defaulting nations, with usually only limited success. Often the companies insist on some kind of insurance or guarantee from their home government before embarking on large arms export deals. Arms sales make up large proportions of the export credits extended in many major arms-exporting countries.

The business of death

The British Export Credits Guarantee Department provides a net subsidy of £222 million ($333 million) a year from the British Government for the British arms industry. Export credit guarantees for arms exports outweigh cover for all other British exports. While the arms trade accounts for only 1.5 per cent of British exports, it has absorbed nearly 40 per cent of export credit guarantee cover over the last five years. In 2007-8, it was 57 per cent.

The picture in Europe is mixed.[8] In Austria no export credit guarantees are given for military sales, and in Switzerland none are given for lethal weapons. In most countries however they are given for arms exports. According to the French Ministry of Finance, around a third of export credit cover provided by the French agency COFACE goes to arms exports.

Other European countries also devote significant proportions of their export credit cover to arms exports. The Netherlands for example (via its agency Atradius-DSB) gave an average of 27 per cent of its export credits to military exports between July 2002 and 2006, with a peak of 57 per cent in 2004. The Belgian export credit agency, Delcredere, gives export credit cover to around 20 per cent of all its licensed arms exports. Strict comparisons are problematic because of differences in policies and reporting standards between countries. The German export credit agency Hermes devotes up to 10 per cent of its export credits to arms, while in Sweden export credit agency EKN averages around 11 per cent.

The main customers for arms bought with the backing of European export credits are South Africa, Saudi Arabia, Indonesia, South Korea and Turkey. The Belgian export credit agency Delcredere supported arms exports to Nepal during the civil war between the Government and the Maoists (see chapter 4). In December 2003 reports in Belgium emerged that New Lachaussée would get export credits from Delcredere to design and supply machines for an ammunition factory in Tanzania. The $8.86 million cover was granted but a furore in Belgium led to the deal being canceled. Delcredere reimbursed New Lachaussée for its losses. These examples illustrate the problem of governments financially supporting arms exports to countries with human rights and development problems.

Spending distortions – Governments also artificially support their arms industries by distorting their own spending on domestic military purchases. They buy more arms from domestic suppliers than really needed, they pay more than these ought to cost, and they choose domestic arms suppliers even if foreign-made equipment is cheaper and better. In any other industry, World Trade Organization rules and other free-trade legislation would prevent such spending distortions as unfair competition. But the military is exempt from international agreements on trade.

The value of this process in British support for arms exports is around £200 million a year.[9] Politicians and civil servants freely admit their preference for 'buying British' to maintain the British arms industry.

For example in July 2003 the British Government decided to spend £800 million on 20 Hawk trainer aircraft with an option for another 24 (despite the Italian Aermacchi 346 being cheaper and technologically superior to BAES's Hawk). The deal would ultimately be worth £3.5 billion over 25 years. The top official at the Ministry of Defence, Kevin Tebbit, refused to sign off the deal because of value for money concerns but was overruled by Defence Secretary Geoff Hoon. As one of the justifications for choosing Hawk (reckoned to be £1 billion more expensive than the Aermacchi over the lifetime of the deal), Hoon cited assisting future export orders – and two months later BAES secured a £1 billion deal with India to supply 66 Hawk jets.

The business of death

Other subsidies

The above are just three *direct* financial subsidies which governments provide for their arms industries. But there are many different ways that governments *indirectly* financially support their arms industries, and while it is more difficult to quantify this kind of support in concrete terms, the benefits to arms companies can be quite considerable.

Research & Development – Governments spend large portions of their military budgets on R&D of new weapons systems which they contract arms companies to carry out on their behalf.

In 2001, the US Department of Defense gave companies $7.7 billion for R&D activities, a figure which rose to $11.8 billion in 2006. The 'Applied Research and Development Funding' enables them to undertake research projects to develop 'dual use' technologies.[10]

The arms-export-related portion of British R&D funding for arms manufacturers amounts to a subsidy of up to £483 million a year for the British arms industry.[11]

Governments justify this expenditure by arguing that it will produce better weapons systems for domestic armed forces, and that costs will be recouped by levying an appropriate charge on exports of the new weapons systems.

The argument is suspect for a number of reasons. Extra charges cannot just be added onto the cost of equipment for export, because the arms export business is such a competitive one – the market forces weapons systems to be exported at near marginal cost.

Also, weapons systems developed with government money are designed and built specifically to meet that government's needs, and often require major modifications (and therefore more cost) before export.

Other methods of indirect subsidy – these include giving away still useful 'surplus' arms to foreign governments as sweeteners to buy other products; and offering grants and subsidies to help arms producers merge or enter into joint partnerships.

Joint production and offsets

Quite apart from the amount of subsidies that governments provide, directly or indirectly, to their arms industries, there are other characteristics of the arms trade which belie the argument that selling arms is good for national economies and employment.

The first is that, increasingly, arms-purchasing countries insist on joint and licensed production of weapons systems. Foreign governments also want to create jobs in their local economies, so they arrange for part or even all of the systems to be built locally. Arms companies are often happy to oblige, since most sales go to developing or middle-income countries where labor can be cheaper and employment standards lower than the corporation would face at home. While some domestic jobs are certainly created or sustained by large weapons contracts, the export of weapons increasingly involves the export of jobs.

Look, for example, at some of BAES's recent big aircraft sales. The Hawks to India deal involves 42 of the 66 Hawks being built under license in India. The air defense variant Tornadoes supplied to Saudi Arabia under the Al Yamamah contracts of the mid-1980s are now being replaced by 72 Eurofighter Typhoon aircraft under the Project Salam. The first 24 planes will be built at BAES's Warton facility in Lancashire, with the remainder likely to be assembled in Saudi Arabia.

Jobs in the arms industry

Offset deals and joint procurement aside, a further

argument – that the weapons business is a thriving employer – is also false. In Britain for example, the number of jobs in the arms industry has fallen from 360,000 in 1994/5 to 315,000 in 2005/6 (with arms export jobs down from 90,000 to 55,000).[12]

Moreover, the argument that a government should spend huge amounts of money propping up an industry to safeguard a relatively small number of jobs is one that only has so much credibility. Governments should no more subsidize their arms business than any other industry to safeguard jobs. Samuel Brittan, the British economist and journalist, has in the past written extensively on the weakness of the employment argument.

He says the argument is based on the myth that there is a 'lump of labor' that is engaged in making specific products, that cannot be deployed elsewhere. If arms orders are lost, those people become unemployed and unemployable, runs the line.

Brittan has pointed out that millions of people change jobs, find jobs or leave jobs every year. He has also written 'people who have spent their lives in a limited skill such as mining are surely more difficult to retrain and move than people who have the more general engineering skills required in the manufacture of arms, aircraft or heavy capital goods'.[13]

A report by the British Ministry of Defence and York University, published in 2001, revealed that 49,000 arms export jobs would be replaced by 67,000 civilian posts if arms exports were cut by half, albeit at a lower average salary per job.[14]

In the popular mind, the jobs figures are much higher, thanks to the arms industry using grossly inflated figures in its lobbying. For example, when, in 2006, the Saudis were threatening to cancel the Project Salam deal because of the ongoing corruption investigation into BAES, the figure of 50,000 jobs under threat was widely touted in the press. But in fact the Eurofighter consortium had commissioned a report which showed that, on the best case, there were around 11,000 jobs dependent on the Salam deal in the whole of Europe and fewer than 5,000 in Britain.

A case study of the redundancies made by BAe in Prestwick in the 1990s, cited in the *Escaping the Subsidy Trap* report, revealed what creative thinking and investment could lead to. A Government task force launched to assist economic development in the light of job losses 'operated until December 1998, by which time the Government announced that 90 per cent of the people laid off by British Aerospace had secured alternative employment locally, and 600 additional jobs in the area had been created'.[15]

So why do governments subsidize their arms industries?

So if arms do not really create jobs nor bring significant amounts of money into national economies, why do governments spend so much propping up the industry?

The answer is perhaps the hardest challenge which anti-arms trade activists face. Countries have a right to defend themselves, the argument runs, and government subsidy for the arms industry means they have the ability to buy weapons to do that. Citing possible future threats, governments argue they need to maintain a Defense Industrial Base (DIB).

The DIB is the ability of a country to manufacture, internally, the weapons and equipment necessary to arm their own military. Governments need to reckon on being able to arm themselves if they become cut off from overseas suppliers. They argue, for the same reason, that they need to retain the technical expertise to build higher specification weapons in the future.

Governments support their arms industries so that in a time of crisis, the industry and the technological expertise still exists in the country and can provide for the country's military needs. By promoting and subsidizing exports, a strong domestic arms industry can be maintained.

This is a much-simplified explanation. Other reasons governments support their industries are because a strong arms industry is seen as a symbol of power in world affairs, because the arms industry has strong lobbying influence, and because politicians like to argue that they are safeguarding jobs since this wins them votes.

In practise, countries do tend to prefer their own industries when making decisions about what to buy for their own military.

The American arms industry's biggest customer is the US military, and so on across all major arms exporting countries, though BAES's biggest customer is the US Department of Defense, because of the sheer quantity and value of arms that the US buys.

As noted in chapter 2, through organizations like OCCAR, some in the EU aim to create a DIB on a European scale. Currently, however, the EU countries are continuing to maintain their own DIBs by subsidizing and supporting their domestic arms industries.

Anti-arms trade campaigners have a number of arguments in response to the standard government position. They contend that the subsidies are so large that they are not a small price to pay for a DIB which is not necessarily needed in today's world; that skewed government support for arms exports leads to other undesirable effects, not least human right abuses and conflict proliferation; that the policy can lead to poor standards of weaponry and an inefficient arms industry; and that diversification from arms manufacture into civil industry would be more productive in the long term (see chapter 9).

Mercenaries: the dogs of war

Selling arms is one side; purchasing people to use them is another. The use of privately hired might is nothing new. The Romans used mercenaries, and the practice probably went back even before them. Italian merchants in the 16th century hired muscle to protect their assets and control trade routes. Colonial explorers were accompanied by hired fighters. From the mid-20th century, Western firms setting up mines and oil exploration in Africa, Asia and Latin America protected their assets by hiring armed heavies.

More recent examples would include Mike Hoare, who attempted a coup in the Congo in the early 1960s and one in the Seychelles in 1982. In 2004, Simon Mann was imprisoned in Zimbabwe for attempting to buy weapons to lead a military coup in Equatorial Guinea. Mann was subsequently extradited to Equatorial Guinea and jailed for 34 years for the conspiracy in 2008.

Mercenaries come under a number of guises, but all include the provision of military might or advice for a profit. Under the guise of 'security' for example, private military companies, consultants, advisors or training outfits, supply all manner of services to both governments and companies, including:
- Direct combat
- Intelligence services
- Training
- Security in conflict zones
- Consulting and planning
- Maintenance and technical assistance
- Operational and logistical support
- Post-conflict reconstruction

Former members of security services often run modern mercenary companies, exploiting their contacts in the arms and political world. They hire disaffected, unemployed former soldiers wherever they win contracts, and source second-hand weapons and equipment for them to fight with. They will often provide whatever services are required, in exchange for hard currency or interests in mining and oil exploration.

The business of death

So how big is the problem? In the last decade there has been a boom in the use of what are called Private Military and Security Companies (PMSCs).[16] This has been driven by the conflict in Iraq.

Current estimates are that there are hundreds of PMSCs operating in more than 50 countries, with a combined revenue of close to $100 billion. Between 2003/4 and 2007/8 the British Government spent £179 million on PMSCs in Iraq and £46 million on PMSCs in Afghanistan.

Why are PMSCs a problem? They are unaccountable. While national armed forces in democratic countries have court martial systems and are accountable through political processes, this does not apply to PMSCs.

They have been implicated in human rights viola-

PMSCs and Iraq

Iraq, say War on Want, 'is the first conflict fought using PMSCs on a major scale'. PMSCs are the second-largest occupying force in Iraq after the US military. The US Government Accountability Office in the summer of 2006 claimed there were more than 48,000 PMSC employees in Iraq from 181 different companies. By May 2006 at least 428 PMSC employees had been killed in Iraq.

Iraqi contracts boosted the income of British PMSCs from £320 million in 2003 to more than £1.8 billion ($2.7 billion) in 2004. The increase in Aegis's turnover from £554,000 in 2003 to £62 million in 2005 was mainly due to its contracts in Iraq. ArmorGroup has estimated the market for 'protective security services' in Iraq increased from $300 million in 2003 to $900 million just a year later.

PMSCs present lucrative opportunities for service personnel. According to the *Sunday Times*, the British special forces unit, the SAS, was forced to increase pay for its soldiers by 50 per cent to stop the flow of soldiers leaving to join PMSCs.

Brigadier-General Karl Horst from the US Army 3rd Infantry Division, responsible for security in Baghdad in 2005 and 2006, said of PMSCs: 'These guys run loose in this country and do stupid stuff. There's no authority over them, so you can't come down on them hard when they escalate force. They shoot people, and someone else has to deal with the aftermath.'[17] ■

tions. For example, the US army investigations into torture at the Abu Ghraib prison in Iraq, accused employees of Titan and CACI of human rights violations.

Other potential problems include PMSCs allowing governments to circumvent legal obstacles or allowing states to conduct covert foreign policies. For example, the US Congress has restricted the number of US military personnel allowed to operate in Colombia, but the restriction can be circumvented by using PMSCs. PMSCs can also allow governments to get round the 'Vietnam syndrome' problem, where public opinion is unwilling to accept casualties.

Despite the proliferation of mercenary activity, and the problems it causes, no effective international legislation yet exists to regulate it, although several attempts have been made.

A condemnation in 1977 by the Organization of African Unity's Convention for the Elimination of Mercenarism in Africa criticized only those who bear arms against recognized governments. Meanwhile, the 1989 UN International Convention Against the Recruitment, Use, Financing and Training of Mercenaries is so little regarded that none of the five permanent members of the UN Security Council have ratified it.

In Britain, which is one of the countries with a large number of PMSCs, individual mercenary activity is still regulated by an 1870 law. No law covers PMSCs. In 2002 the British Government set out several options for regulating PMSCs, but has done nothing since, referring to the 'considerable value' of PMSCs to the British economy.

Some other countries are taking steps. In 2007 the US House of Representatives passed the Military and Security Contracting Act establishing American legal authority over PMSCs. In Iraq the Government is attempting to remove the immunity from prosecution

PMSCs enjoy there. In Afghanistan the Government has shut down nine PMSCs for operating without a license.

Recent events show there is still a pressing need for action against PMSCs. 2007 saw several documented instances where civilians in Iraq were killed by PMSCs.

Espionage

Private companies have also been linked to espionage against anti-arms trade protesters.

In the mid-1990s a major part of Campaign Against Arms Trade (CAAT)'s campaigning activities was lobbying against the sale of Hawk aircraft to Indonesia by BAe. In 2003 the *Sunday Times* published a major exposé of the activities of a company called Threat Response International, run by a woman named Evelyn Le Chene. Information received by the newspaper suggested she had from 1996 to 1999 been covertly gathering information on CAAT for BAE.

Le Chene, who is alleged to have run agents in CAAT as well as gaining access to IT systems and supporter databases, submitted a substantial number of reports to BAe about CAAT's activities, covering a wide range of activities including parliamentary lobbying, meetings and direct actions.

When Le Chene's activities were exposed by the newspaper, an internal CAAT investigation revealed a member of staff, Martin Hogbin, had been forwarding large numbers of emails from CAAT to a company unknown to CAAT. Hogbin resigned before the investigation could go further, though he did admit forwarding the emails. Hogbin, who by his own admission had previously worked in the arms industry, had joined CAAT as a volunteer in spring 1997 and the paid staff in November 2001.

After investigating, the Information Commissioner later told CAAT that the recipient of Hogbin's emails, many of which contained confidential information, was a company linked to Evelyn Le Chene. In 2007, BAES admitted in legal correspondence that it had received information from Evelyn Le Chene.[18]

Four years on from the allegations in the *Sunday Times*, it emerged that BAES had paid another private investigator to collect material about CAAT. In January 2007, BAES's solicitors told CAAT's lawyers they had received an email containing legal advice CAAT had been given about its attempt to overturn in the courts the Serious Fraud Office's decision to drop a corruption investigation against BAES.

CAAT successfully applied for an injunction against BAES which forced BAES to reveal that the source of the email was Paul Mercer, a private investigator, whose company Ligne Deux Associates was paid for 'media and internet monitoring' information about CAAT. CAAT took legal action against BAES, who were made to promise 'not to intercept by any unlawful means... [and] not to solicit, voluntarily receive or procure any confidential communication or document' belonging to CAAT.

CAAT is not the only peace organization that has suffered in this way. In the US, an investigation by *Mother Jones* has alleged that Mary Lou Sapone 'has covertly infiltrated citizens groups for private security firms hired by corporations that are targeted by activist campaigns'. *Mother Jones* alleged that Sapone, who was heavily involved in gun control pressure groups, worked for the National Rifle Association, the leading pro-gun lobby in the US.[19]

1 Much of the information in this section is taken from *Who calls the shots? How government-corporate collusion drives arms exports*, Campaign Against Arms Trade, Feb 2005. **2** www.newamerica.net/publications/articles/2008/time_end_waste_pentagon_7367 **3** Much of the information in this section is taken from www.armsfairs.com **4** Defence, Foreign Affairs, International Development and Trade and Industry Committees, *Strategic Export Controls: Annual Report for 2004, Quarterly Reports for 2005, Licensing Policy and Parliamentary Scrutiny,*

The business of death

House of Commons, 19 Jul 2006, HC873. **5** Paul Ingram and Roy Isbister, *Escaping the Subsidy Trap: Why arms exports are bad for Britain* (BASIC, Oxford Research Group and Saferworld, Sep 2004). **6** Samuel Brittan, *Subsidizing a Deadly Trade*, Campaign Against Arms Trade, Jul 2001. **7** Hansard, 16 Jun 2008. **8** Much of the information in this section is taken from Martin Broek, Marijn Peperkamp, Frank Slijper and Wendela van de Vries, *European Export Credit Agencies and the financing of arms trade*, European Network Against Arms Trade, 2007. **9** See footnote 5. **10** Stephen Slivinski, *The Corporate Welfare State: How the Federal Government Subsidizes US Businesses*, CATO Institute, May 2007. **11** See footnote 5. **12** Steven Schofield, *Making Arms, Wasting Skills*, Campaign Against Arms Trade, Apr 2008. **13** www.samuelbrittan.co.uk/text165_p.html **14** Malcolm Chalmers, Neil V Davies, Keith Hartley and Chris Wilkinson, *The Economic Costs and Benefits of UK Defence Exports*, Centre for Defence Economics, University of York, Research Monograph Series 13, November 2001. **15** See footnote 5. **16** Much of the information in this section is taken from Fabien Mathieu and Nick Dearden, *Corporate Mercenaries: The threat of private military and security companies*, War on Want, Nov 2006. **17** War on Want, *Getting Away With Murder: The need for action on UK Private Military and Security Companies*, Feb 2008. **18** The information below is taken from the account by comedian Mark Thomas at www.guardian.co.uk/world/2007/dec/04/bae.armstrade **19** The full investigation can be viewed at http://tinyurl.com/66orm5

7 Corruption

Why corruption in the arms trade is so rife... Government complicity... Al Yamamah and other corruption investigations.

IN RECENT YEARS, the issue of corruption in the arms trade has become increasingly prominent. This is largely because of the allegations made against BAES, accused of paying massive bribes to win arms deals abroad. There have been criminal investigations into BAES in several countries.

Joe Roeber is a British author and a member of the Strategy Committee of Transparency International (TI)'s Defence Against Corruption project, which aims to 'combat corruption in one of the most corruption-prone of all business sectors, the international official arms trade'. Roeber has written that the arms trade is 'hard-wired for corruption'.[1] It is a highly secretive business done behind closed doors. Government officials and arms company executives, from both buying and selling countries, go about their business away from the public eye, hiding behind the veils of national security and commercial confidentiality.

Why is corruption a problem?
Corruption is the abuse of public or private office for personal gain. It is, effectively, theft. When someone in a government takes a bribe, for instance, they are diverting money that could be spent for the benefit of the people of the country into their back pocket.

Corruption is a massive global problem. According to the British Government, every year around $1 trillion is paid in bribes around the world.

The World Bank has identified corruption as 'among the greatest obstacles to economic and social development. It undermines development by distorting the rule of law and weakening the institutional foundation on which economic growth depends'. The Organization for Economic Co-operation and Development (OECD), a group of leading industrial nations, has said 'corruption is the primary threat to good governance, sustainable economic development, democratic process and fair business practices'.

Corruption has a particularly severe impact on developing countries, which, as we have seen, are the 'primary focus of foreign arms sales activity by weapons suppliers'.

The UNDP says: 'The negative impact of corruption on development is no longer questioned. Evidence from across the globe confirms that corruption impacts the poor disproportionately. Corruption hinders economic development, reduces social services, and diverts investments in infrastructure, institutions and social services. Moreover, it fosters an anti-democratic environment characterized by uncertainty, unpredictability and declining moral values and disrespect for constitutional institutions and authority. It also undermines efforts to achieve the MDGs. Corruption therefore reflects a democracy, human rights and governance deficit that negatively impacts poverty and human security.'

The arms trade, bribery and corruption

Roeber has talked to arms trade insiders about corruption. They confirm that it is standard practice to bribe in arms deals.

The US Commerce Department collects complaints from US companies about unfair competition from bribery by their competitors in overseas markets. The latest available figures from 2000 show more than half of all reports concern arms or military equipment deals. The arms trade is possibly the most corrupt of all legal trades.

The payment of 'commissions' (a common euphemism for bribes) of one sort or another is widespread in international business. Until recently, the payment of 'commissions' was even granted as a tax-free expense by many Western governments. The Trade and Industry Select Committee of Britain's House of Commons has written 'the payment of commission or fees to agents is generally recognized to be a common method of paying bribes'.[2]

Bribery and commissions are close cousins, but must be separated. Business 'agents' who take 'commission' can and do perform perfectly legitimate services for the companies they work for. They can provide an additional source of information for companies, monitor the activities of competitors, and promote their company's equipment and services. But what makes a 'commission' a 'bribe' is its purpose. If it is not to reimburse the agent for legitimate expenses, but so the agent can pay someone to influence a decision on a contract, then the 'commission' is a 'bribe'. Typical signs that a 'commission' is a corrupt payment are when they are extremely high, are paid by an agent to officials with influence, or to those with interests in seeing an arms deal taking place.

Bribes (typically paid via 'agents') can be in the form of visible cash payments to officials, generals and government ministers; or in the form of gifts like expensive cars, gems or other in-kind donations.

Roeber has identified the structural causes that make the international arms trade so corrupt relative to other legal commercial activities:

• The arms industry faces continued over-capacity in production, meaning competition between arms firms is fiercer than in other industries. Moreover, major arms deals are very large in value but few in number. Each might make the difference between life and death for the arms companies. It is a high-stakes game.
• In the developing world, power often rests in the hands of an unaccountable political élite.
• There is a lack of price transparency. Arms sales

are large, complex and each country has different requirements. Price comparison is near impossible and hence the prices can be manipulated so that they are 'padded' with 'commissions'.

• Arms sales relate to 'national security' and thus secrecy surrounds them. The resulting lack of accountability provides a fertile breeding ground for corruption.

Why is arms trade corruption a particular problem? Bribes can motivate corrupt leaders to make superfluous arms purchases because they carry a kickback. As Roeber has argued, corruption adds to the arms race, providing government buyers with incentives to buy more weapons than they require, and even in some cases, than they have the military personnel to cope with.

State complicity

As we have seen, governments are intimately involved in the arms trade. And as corruption is central to the arms trade, governments are often complicit in the corrupt practices.

In the last few years, historical evidence has come to light which shows that the Government of one of the leading arms-exporting countries, Britain, has been fully aware of the corrupt nature of the arms trade for many years.[3] But because Britain was determined, as former Labour Minister Denis Healey put it, to 'secure [our] rightful share' of the global arms market, it ignored it. Sadly, the British Government still prefers to do this today.

Prior to the mid-1970s, the British Government was heavily involved in the corruption that was rife in international arms deals. The Ministry of Defence (MoD), when selling surplus weapons or weapons produced by nationalized companies, directly employed agents in the expectation that they would indulge in bribery.

Official policy was to turn a blind eye. When the British Embassy in Caracas became squeamish about involvement in corrupt transactions, an MoD official wrote: 'I am completely mystified by just what your problem is… people who deal with the arms trade, even if they are sitting in a government office, live day by day with this sort of activity, and equally day by day they carry out transactions knowing that at some point bribery is involved. Obviously I and my colleagues in this office do not ourselves engage in it, but we believe that various people who are somewhere along the chain of our transactions do. They do not tell us what they are doing and we do not enquire. We are interested in the end result'.

On occasion, British Embassy officials got mixed up in corrupt transactions. For example, in 1968 the Defense Attaché at the Jeddah Embassy passed on a bribe request from a top Saudi general to the arms company Vickers, who were hoping to sell their tanks to the Saudi Army.

Bribery was seen as the natural way of the world overseas. A senior British Foreign and Commonwealth Office official wrote in 1977: 'It is common knowledge in Middle Eastern posts that business firms are likely to have to do some palm-greasing if they are to get contracts… bribery in many countries – to a greater or less extent – is part of the local way of life. 'Bribery and corruption' at home is of course our business; abroad it is primarily the business of the government and society concerned'. If British companies' actions were investigated, 'our exports seem bound to suffer. So, too, will our relations with influential foreigners who have been involved'.[4] As we will see in the Al Yamamah case, such attitudes are still well represented in the higher echelons of the British Government.

Watering down anti-corruption rules

In recent years, the British Government has continued to be reluctant to clamp down on arms trade corruption. However, in 1997, the OECD drew up a set of standards to combat the bribing of officials in international business transactions, which 34 leading exporting countries, including Britain, signed.

In Britain, the Export Credits Guarantee Department (ECGD) provides companies with insurance against foreign governments defaulting on their payments. In the mid-1970s a Cabinet Committee was told that ECGD 'occasionally come upon particular instances of questionable payments', but as it was 'impracticable to investigate the commercial morality of business submitted',[5] they did 'not enquire whether any part of the commission may be in the nature of a bribe'.[6]

In September 2000 ECGD abandoned the previous 'laissez-faire approach to corruption' and introduced new anti-bribery procedures which were tougher than those prescribed by the OECD.[7] In May 2004 the procedures were further strengthened.

ECGD's major 'customer' companies (including BAES, Rolls Royce and Airbus) objected. A sustained lobbying campaign was co-ordinated by the industry lobbying group the Confederation of British Industry (CBI). ECGD excluded NGOs from discussions about proposed changes the companies were asking for. In November 2004 ECGD brought in revised procedures which substantially weakened the anti-bribery provisions.

The issue was new ECGD rules requiring exporters to disclose the identities of intermediaries when they applied for financial support from the taxpayer. The companies did not want to tell ECGD who their agents were. ECGD officials attempted to resist the corporate lobbying but were overruled by the Cabinet Minister, Patricia Hewitt. She agreed that the companies did not have to give the names or addresses of these intermediaries, provided the firms gave an explanation.[8]

The Corner House, an NGO known for its anti-corruption work, mounted a Judicial Review challenge in the High Court. They argued that the Government had failed to follow its own policy on consultation with stakeholders, and that the Government should not have made changes merely at industry's behest. In January 2005, just as a two-day hearing was to begin, ECGD settled out of court. It agreed to open a full public consultation on the changes to its anti-corruption rules.

In March 2006, the ECGD reinstated its rules that companies who want ECGD insurance have to reveal the identity of agents used to make payments abroad.[9]

This episode is important, not only because the arms trade is the most corrupt of all international trades, but also because, as we have seen, ECGD gives a disproportionately large share of its support to arms companies relative to civil exports. Indeed, what is extraordinary is the extent to which ECGD's business is focused on just one contract – the Al Yamamah and Salam deals with Saudi Arabia. A Freedom of Information request by CAAT discovered this was a £750 million guarantee given to BAES and renewed every year. ECGD told CAAT that in 2006/07 it was the only military contract it underwrote, and its annual report showed that it accounted for an astonishing 42 per cent of all guarantees issued in that year. BAES terminated the cover for Al Yamamah and Project Salam in September 2008.

The Al Yamamah corruption investigation

Thankfully, there is a growing recognition that corruption is a bad thing in international business. There are attempts being made to rein it in.

For 25 years, the US has had anti-corruption legislation on the statute books. The 1977 Foreign Corrupt Practices Act (FCPA) bans payments to foreign officials, and to a large extent keeps corruption in US arms deals in check. But ironically, because, until recently, few other countries had similar legislation, some have argued the move has led to proliferation of corruption in non-US companies as they attempt to compete with more sophisticated US weapons systems.

The OECD treaty on bribery has been slow to produce positive change. According to Transparency International, as of June 2008, only eight countries had passed new legislation that would help improve enforcement of anti-bribery laws.[10] Britain in particular has dragged its feet, arguing that national legislation already covers the issues addressed. But pressure from the US, following the 11 September 2001 attacks, led Britain to introduce monitoring of money channels as part of its controversial Anti-Terrorism Act, which came into force in 2002.

Under the OECD treaty, Britain has promised that prosecutions of bribery 'shall not be influenced by considerations of national economic interest, the potential effect upon relations with another State or the identity of the natural or legal persons involved'.

However, the flaw in the OECD code is that it

What is Al Yamamah?

Al Yamamah, which means 'the Dove' in Arabic, was Britain's biggest arms deal, and kept BAES afloat for more than two decades.

It is a government-to-government deal. The MoD manages a sub-contract with BAES who provide the equipment and services to the Saudi Government.

The deal started in September 1985 when a Memorandum of Understanding (MoU) was signed by the two Governments. The detailed arrangements were set out in an MoU agreed in February 1986. An extension to the program was agreed in an MoU signed in July 1988.

Initially BAe sold the Royal Saudi Air Force 48 Tornado ground attack aircraft, 24 Tornado air defense aircraft, 30 Hawk ground attack/trainer aircraft, and 30 PC-9 training aircraft. The aircraft came with support services, equipment, weapons, ammunition and electronic warfare systems. More equipment was bought in 1993, following the 1988 agreement.

Under Al Yamamah BAe provided support for the equipment it had sold. This arrangement continues today under a new name. At the end of 2006 Al Yamamah became the Saudi British Defence Co-operation Programme (SBDCP). ■

is to be controlled and policed by governments. This problem is graphically illustrated by the hugely controversial investigation into allegations of corruption surrounding Britain's biggest arms deal: the Al Yamamah deal with Saudi Arabia.

Within a fortnight of the signing of the Al Yamamah MoU in September 1985, allegations of bribes were made in an Arabic news sheet stating that 'four cavaliers' had taken £600 million in commission on the deal.[11]

No evidence to substantiate these claims (denied at the time) ever emerged. But 20 years later, circumstantial evidence was discovered which suggests large commissions were possible.

Files accidentally released into Britain's National Archives in May 2006 and discovered by the author revealed a dramatic price increase during the deal's negotiation.[12] It is common in arms deals for the prices of weapons to be raised so that commissions can be skimmed off the top. The difference in the price from the original quote in 1984 to the final price in 1986 equated to around a £600 million price rise for the aircraft on the deal.

The British Government took no action to investigate. Other allegations of corruption around Al Yamamah have been made over the years, some reported in the previous edition of this book. These have included allegations of payments to well-connected individuals, and 'commissions' being paid on parts for the Tornado aircraft. But, the allegations have all been denied, not documented and easily brushed aside.

However, in 2001 Edward Cunningham, a former employee of Robert Lee International (RLI), made allegations to the Serious Fraud Office (SFO) that RLI was running a 'slush fund' for Saudi royals. The SFO drew the MoD's attention to this. Not wanting to 'set damaging hares running', the MoD's top official, Kevin Tebbit, asked BAES Chairman Dick Evans about the allegations. Dick Evans told him nothing was wrong.[13] The MoD took no further action.[14]

Two years later *The Guardian* newspaper published a series of exposés about RLI and another company called Travellers World. Travellers World, owned by entrepreneur Peter Gardiner, allegedly ran a 'slush fund' to entertain Prince Turki bin Nasser, the head of the Saudi Air Force, and other top Saudis. Gardiner claimed he had paid around £60 million in bribes between 1989 and 2002, for which he was reimbursed by BAES.[15] BAES dismissed the allegations as 'nine-year-old allegations that are ill-informed and wrong'. It said: 'there is not now and there has never been in existence what the media refers to as a "slush fund"'.[16]

Peter Gardiner approached the SFO in March 2004. In July 2004 the SFO decided to investigate corruption allegations against BAES in Saudi Arabia.[17] It also started investigations into BAES's arms deals with South Africa, Romania, Tanzania, and the Czech Republic (see box, page 108).

Just over a year after the investigation started, in October 2005, the SFO told BAES it had to hand over details of the payments it had made to business agents in connection with its contracts with Saudi Arabia.[18] A long lobbying campaign by BAES and the British Government to force the SFO to abandon the investigation began.

BAES, the suspect in the investigation, called for the investigation to be halted 'in the public interest'. It said that if the SFO carried on it would damage the British Government's relationship with Saudi Arabia and BAES's chances of winning contracts in Saudi Arabia. The request, supported by the British Government, was rejected by the SFO.

In July 2006 the SFO were said to be looking into payments made to various Swiss bank accounts in relation to BAES's Saudi contracts. The Saudi Government told the British Government there would be dire consequences if the investigation continued.

At the time the MoD and BAES were negotiating a new contract with Saudi Arabia. The Saudis wanted to buy the Eurofighter aircraft from BAES, a deal worth billions. To show their threats about the investigation were genuine, in September 2006, the Saudis walked away from the talks. So again the British Government asked the SFO to halt the investigation. The SFO again refused.

The Saudis had said they would stop sharing secret intelligence with Britain and abandon co-operation on counter-terrorism. In November 2006 the British Ambassador to Saudi Arabia, Sir Sherard Cowper-Coles, told the SFO that 'British lives on British streets were at risk' if the investigation continued. A campaign in the media started to get the investigation halted. In December 2006 reports suggested the Saudis had given the British Government 10 days to stop the investigation or all co-operation would cease. Prime Minister Tony Blair met Attorney General (Lord) Peter Goldsmith on 11 December and demanded the investigation be stopped. On 14 December Goldsmith told Parliament the SFO investigation had been halted because, had it carried on, it would have had 'seriously negative consequences for the United Kingdom public interest in terms of both national security and our highest priority foreign policy objectives in the Middle East'.

The reward for the British Government and BAES came quickly. Negotiations restarted on the Eurofighter contract in January 2007.[19] BAES won the £4.43 billion contract in September. In October 2007 King Abdullah of Saudi Arabia paid a state visit to Britain. It included a state banquet hosted by the Queen at Buckingham Palace. According to the current British Ambassador to Saudi Arabia, Sir William Patey, it was the 'high point' of Anglo-Saudi relations in 2007. He said in March 2008 that relations between Britain and Saudi Arabia were as close as they had ever been.[20]

A legal challenge to the decision by the SFO to stop

the investigation was made by two pressure groups, CAAT and The Corner House. In April 2008 the High Court ruled that the decision to end the investigation was unlawful. The SFO appealed to Britain's highest court, the House of Lords. The Law Lords ruled in favor of the SFO in July 2008. The investigation will therefore remain closed forever.

The case revealed the immense strength of the arms

Other investigations of BAES[21]

Tanzania

Tanzania bought a military air defense radar system from BAES in 2001 for £28 million, saying it could also be used for civilian air traffic control. Being a poor country, Tanzania had to borrow from British bank Barclays to buy the radar.

The World Bank and the International Civil Aviation Organization attacked the purchase as unnecessary and expensive. Clare Short, International Development Secretary, tried to stop the deal, but was overruled by Prime Minister Tony Blair.

Allegations, which BAES deny, were made that a commission of 30 per cent of the radar's price was made into a Swiss account via intermediaries. The SFO and Tanzania's anti-corruption bureau have investigated the deal.

Czech Republic

The Czechs agreed to lease Gripen fighter planes for £400 million in 2004. BAES leased the planes in a joint venture with Swedish company Saab.

Swedish TV alleged that BAES made secret payments to agents of more than £4 million. The three agents named, and BAES, denied that any of this money was for bribes.

The US authorities were the first to allege corruption. The SFO in London began to investigate in 2004. Investigations were also launched by Sweden, Austria and the Czech Republic, as individuals in each country were said to be involved.

Romania

Two surplus British frigates, HMS London and HMS Coventry, were sold to Romania in 2003. It was a government-to-government deal organized by the MoD. They were sold for the scrap price of £100,000 each.

BAES were paid £116 million by Romania to refurbish the ships and industry's vested interests. A foreign government was able to interfere successfully with the British justice system to stop a criminal investigation of a British arms company. Effectively this means the OECD anti-bribery treaty is unenforceable in Britain. The OECD reported that the British Government made no serious attempt to stop the Saudi Government behaving in this way, nor was the importance of upholding the rule of

---

maintain them. Romania had to borrow the money from Deutsche Bank, in a loan guaranteed by ECGD.

Allegations, which BAES deny, were made that an agent was secretly paid £7 million to fix the deal. The SFO investigation involved police raids at the agent's flat in Chelsea.

South Africa

South Africa is a country with severe financial and social problems that is still a major arms importer. In 1997, nearly 20 per cent of the adult population was illiterate, and roughly 50 per cent were unemployed. Despite chronic poverty, the Government, under Thabo Mbeki, announced in 1999 that it would embark on a major rearmament of the South African National Defence Force.

The program includes the purchase of 52 fighter planes from a BAES and Saab consortium, patrol boats and submarines from German-led consortia and 40 light helicopters from the Italian firm Agusta.

When it was first arranged, the rearmament was valued at between $5-6 billion. The cost was twice the country's housing budget and ten times the amount set aside to deal with HIV/AIDS, two of its most severe development problems. Before the contracts were finalized, South Africa's treasury warned the Government that the purchases would be risky and would use up much of recent public spending increases.

The deal, which British Prime Minister Tony Blair lobbied for, was backed by ECGD to the tune of £1.6 billion ($2.4 billion).

There have been convictions from this deal (not connected to BAES). Tony Yengeni and Schabir Shaikh have been jailed for involvement in bribery.

Leaked evidence from the South African police, published in *The Guardian* newspaper, suggests BAES is accused of 'financially incentivising' South African politicians by paying £100 million, partly via its agent John Bredenkamp.[22] Bredenkamp and BAES deny the allegations and the investigation continues. ■

law much in evidence in the British Government's considerations about where the 'public interest' lay. In fact, less than a year after the Saudis had threatened the British Government, King Abdullah was given the red carpet treatment of a state visit. Such is the commitment of the British Government to maintaining the arms trade with the Saudis, and BAES's influence at the heart of the British Government.

1 Much of the material in the next three pages is from Joe Roeber, *Parallel Markets: Corruption in the International Arms Trade*, Campaign Against Arms Trade, 2005. **2** Trade and Industry Select Committee, *Implementation of ECGD's Business Principles*, House of Commons, 8 Mar 2005, HC374-1. **3** The material in this section is taken from Nicholas Gilby, 'The United Kingdom's Ministry of Defence and the bribe culture,' in *The Economics of Peace and Security Journal*, vol 3, no1, 2008. **4** Minute from RS Faber to Mr Kerr, 20 May 1977, File FCO 69/592, The National Archives. **5** Cabinet Paper GEN 11(76)1 'International Business Practice', Apr 1976, File CAB 130/859, The National Archives. **6** Enclosure to letter from J Hobson to C Brearley, 23 April 1976, File DEFE 68/110, The National Archives. **7** The material in this section is taken from R (Corner House Research) v Secretary of State for Trade and Industry, [2005] EWCA Civ 92, paragraphs 82-132. See http://tinyurl.com/c3blor **8** *The Guardian*, 25 Jan 2005. **9** Ibid. **10** Fritz Heimann and Gillian Dell, *Progress Report 2008: Enforcement of the OECD Convention on Combating Bribery of Foreign Public Officials*, Transparency International, 24 Jun 2008. **11** Letter from PF Ricketts, FCO, to CD Powell, No 10, 10 October 1985, available at http://tinyurl.com/cve9n9 **12** Riyadh Telegram No.ZMC/ ZDK/ZBG/A2P of 6 Jan 1986 to MoD, available at http://tinyurl.com/cyadka. **13** *The Guardian*, 10 Sep 2003 and 13 Oct 2003. Hansard, 19 Jan 2004, Col 921W. **14** Letter from Geoffrey Hoon to Gavin Strang MP, 26 Jan 2004, copy on file at CAAT. **15** *The Sunday Times*, 25 Jul 2004. **16** BBC News website, 5 Oct 2004. See http://news.bbc.co.uk/1/hi/business/3712770.stm **17** Hansard, 1 May 2008, Col 574W. **18** This section is based on the author's personal knowledge and documents disclosed in the Judicial Review case R (Corner House Research and Campaign Against Arms Trade) v Director of the Serious Fraud Office, [2008] EWHC 714 (Admin). Documents are available at www.thecornerhouse.org.uk/ subject/corruption/ **19** On 6 Jan 2007 Prince Sultan, the Saudi Defense Minister, said he was looking forward to taking delivery of the BAE Eurofighters 'soon'. See http://news.bbc.co.uk/1/hi/business/6182137.stm. **20** See Information Tribunal case *Campaign Against Arms Trade vs Information Commissioner and Ministry of Defence*. Transcript of hearing 3 Mar 2008, available at www.caat.org. uk/infotribunal/transcript-2008-03-03.pdf **21** Further information is available at www.guardian.co.uk/baefiles/page/0,,2095864,00.html **22** *The Guardian*, 6 Dec 2008.

8 Attempts at control

Small arms, their producers and exporters... Murky markets... Landmines and cluster bombs... The trade in torture equipment... Arms brokering.

FORTUNATELY IT IS not all doom and gloom. A significant body of people is trying to do something about the arms trade. Understandably, efforts have been focused on some of the worst aspects of the arms trade, such as the manufacture and trade in small arms, land-mines, cluster bombs and torture equipment. One of the most serious problems is the lethal trade in small arms.

Small arms and light weapons require a special mention in any assessment of the global trade in armaments, simply because they are so prolific, the trade in them is so difficult to control and the devas-

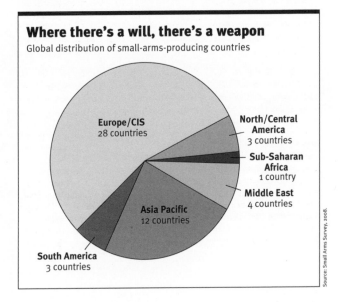

Where there's a will, there's a weapon

Global distribution of small-arms-producing countries

Europe/CIS
28 countries

North/Central America
3 countries

Sub-Saharan Africa
1 country

Middle East
4 countries

Asia Pacific
12 countries

South America
3 countries

Source: Small Arms Survey, 2008.

tation caused by them is so severe.

Taking the definition of the UN panel of government experts on small arms, the category includes all of the following military, police and domestic weapons: revolvers and self-loading pistols, rifles and carbines, assault rifles, sub-machine guns and light machine guns, heavy machine guns, hand-held under-barrel and mounted grenade launchers, portable anti-tank and anti-aircraft guns, recoilless rifles, portable launchers of anti-tank and anti-aircraft systems, and mortars of less than 100 mm caliber.[1]

There are plenty of them, and they are everywhere. They are used by police and security patrols, by national armies and by guerrilla and revolutionary groups, they are carried by civilians legally in a number of countries, for sport in many more, and illegally in every country. They feature in practically every armed conflict between nation-states, in internal and civil wars, in gang fighting and as status symbols.

They are so prolific because they are small and relatively cheap, easy to pass on, smuggle, hide, steal, capture from an enemy or buy over the counter. But they are also ubiquitous because of the sheer numbers they are produced in: thousands of them, every day, all over the world. It is a myth that the trade in small arms is only one of recycling second- and third-hand weapons. New production merely creates more second- and third-hand guns.

The *Small Arms Survey* estimates between 7.5 and 8 million small arms are produced every year, and that 'more than 1,200 companies in at least 90 countries are involved in some aspect of small arms and light weapons production'.[2] China, Russia and the US remain the three main producers, though the EU as a whole is also a major producer. In all, at least 30 countries are considered by the *Small Arms Survey* to be significant producers.

The *Survey* is a project of the Graduate Institute of

International Studies in Geneva, which has attempted to profile and estimate the proliferation of firearms (hand-held guns and rifles, rather than hand-held missile launchers and the like), based on rough estimates and incomplete reporting by countries.

The nature of small arms, and the nature of the traffic in them – legal, illegal, underground market, civilian, smuggled, home-made – means there can never be precise data on which countries have the most of them, or which of these are legal, illegal, military or civilian.

Their latest research estimates that there are at least 639 million small arms and light weapons in the world today – at least one gun for every 10 of the world's people. Over half of all of these are privately owned.

Dirty dozen

The main exporters of small arms, according to the *Small Arms Survey,* are Russia, the US, Italy, Germany, Brazil and China. Other important exporters for whom there is little reliable data are reported to be Bulgaria, Iran, Israel, North Korea, Pakistan and Singapore. Innumerable independent arms dealers, criminals, brokers and intermediaries control the illicit trade.

Some governments and campaigners draw a distinction between legally transferred small arms and the illegal trade.

Small arms, huge impact
According to the Small Arms Survey:

Between 60 and 90 per cent of direct conflict deaths in the world are as a result of the use of small arms and light weapons.

Between 200,000 and 270,000 non-conflict-related firearm deaths occur in the world each year. Two in five of all murders involve firearms.

Firearm injuries cost society more than other kinds of violent wound. Medical treatment of a firearm injury in Brazil and Colombia, for example, costs between 1.7 and three times more than that of a stab wound. ■

Attempts at control

Worldwide, the 'legal' trade makes up by far the majority of small arms sales. The annual legal global trade in small arms and light weapons is estimated at $4 billion. This represents transfers of arms to police services, military and security forces as well as to the domestic and sporting market.

Without the legal trade in weapons, the illegal trade would not exist. It can be argued that all legal small arms transfers should be of concern to campaigners for a number of reasons.

As with the transfer of tanks, planes and bombs, the trade in light weapons between governments is a problem if these are used to perpetrate human rights abuses. For instance, see the case of Nepal, detailed in chapter 4.

Another problem is that when armed forces buy new weapons, their older ones often cascade into the semi-legal (gray) trade or into the illegal trade. (The US 'right to bear arms' market for domestic weapons is the main source of illegal weapon ownership there). As more weapons clatter onto the market, whether legal or illegal, the cheaper they become – and so the more readily available to rebel fighters, civilians and even children.

Likewise, legally transferred weapons find their way onto the illegal market through other means: corrupt officials, the looting of arms stockpiles (for example, during civil unrest in Albania in 1997[3]) and poor security measures.

Murky markets

The semi-legal (gray) and black markets in light arms have received disproportionate concern from politicians and campaigners alike. There is no doubt that it is the illegal arms market that is the driving force behind civil conflicts, corruption, crime and random violence but, as described above, they really owe their strength to the legal trade.

Oxfam has cited reports by UN Panels of Experts on

African countries under UN arms embargoes showing that companies and individuals in a large number of countries have enabled the illegal acquisition of arms and ammunition.[4] These countries include Albania, Belgium, the British Virgin Islands, Britain, Bulgaria, Burkina Faso, Burundi, the Cayman Islands, Côte d'Ivoire, Cyprus, Egypt, Gibraltar, Guinea, Israel, Liberia, Libya, Moldova, Nigeria, Romania, Russia, Rwanda, Serbia, South Africa, Togo, Uganda, Ukraine, United Arab Emirates and Zimbabwe.

The 'gray' market refers to transfers of light weapons that are only on the edge of legality. It encompasses those supplied covertly to rebel forces by governments with an interest in their success (for example, according to Oxfam, 'several states in the Great Lakes Region and Horn of Africa have been accused in various UN Sanctions Panel reports of facilitating transfers of ammunition to armed groups in neighboring states'[5]), or transfers struck via arms brokers who exploit loopholes in arms control legislation to make sales of second-hand weapons stockpiled from finished conflicts on the other side of the world.

The illegal trade is easier to define, but is much harder to quantify, by its very nature. Black market transfers are made in clear violation of national and international laws, without permission or consent from governments.

The small arms market, with its legal, gray and black constituents, is the murkiest market of all: this is precisely what makes it so hard to monitor, control and ultimately attempt to abolish. Below are two recent examples.[6]

Baghdad's black markets – As Oxfam has argued, the death toll in Iraq since the 2003 invasion 'is fueled by the easy availability of small arms and ammunition'. When Saddam Hussein's regime was toppled in 2003, around 20 million weapons were estimated to be in

Iraq. The *Small Arms Survey* has argued that the failure of the coalition forces to secure stockpiles in the early days of the conflict and their early disbanding of the Iraqi army are the main reasons why small arms are so easily available in Iraq.

Research by the Iraqi NGO Doctors for Iraq has found black market ammunition for 9mm pistols and AK assault rifles comes from Bulgaria, China, the Czech Republic, Hungary, Romania, Russia and Serbia.

Some, of course, was produced many years ago, but the NGO found significant evidence that newly imported ammunition was becoming increasingly widespread. It suggested two probable explanations: smuggling, and leakage from coalition supplies to the new Iraqi security forces set up after Saddam's overthrow.

The latter explanation gained credibility with the publication by the US Government Accountability Office in 2007 of a report which said that the US Government could not account for at least 190,000 weapons (110,000 AK-47 assault rifles and 80,000 pistols) transferred from the US Government to the Iraqi security forces.[7] In 2006, 20,000 Beretta pistols were shipped from Italy to Iraq via Britain. One of the brokers involved said: 'Some police, I presume, are corrupt, and they sell them on the black market. Some of these Berettas have turned up in the hands of wrong people and it's opened the lid on it. Because Iraq is in such a mess, there must be kit flying all over the place. Everyone must be at it.'[8]

The diversion of weapons is a major problem. In Iraq, according to Amnesty: 'US-sponsored systems of outsourcing and sub-contracting for arms supplies to Iraq have failed to protect against the diversion of weapons... Many of these imported weapons remain unaccounted for and stocks have been diverted to and captured by individuals, militia and armed groups who commit grave human rights abuses.'[9]

Somalia – the background to the conflict is covered in chapter 3, but the trade in small arms has fueled the violence despite the 1992 UN arms embargo. A UN Panel of Experts has reported that once small arms and ammunition arrive in Somalia they are distributed by local dealers to armed groups.

There are almost daily transfers of weapons and ammunition between Yemen and Somalia. Ammunition is important in Somalia and, according to the UN, prices surge on the black market when warlords anticipate future battles and decide to stock up on supplies.

Landmines

Children, whether child soldiers or not, are often the main victims of landmines. In the words of the International Campaign to Ban Landmines: 'Landmines are indiscriminate because a landmine is triggered by its victim, whether military or civilian. Landmines are inhumane because they inflict brutal injuries and have disastrous long-term consequences.' Because they are indiscriminate and the damage they inflict not proportionate to military objectives (because they continue to be active long after conflicts end), 'antipersonnel mines violate international humanitarian law. Like other weapons of their type... they are illegal and can and should be outlawed completely'.[10]

As the NGO Landmine Action says: 'Contamination or even the suspicion of contamination with landmines can deny people access to community resources such as water sources and agricultural land, creating or worsening poverty'.[11]

More than any other weapon of war, landmines have received much public and legislative attention over recent decades. In December 1997, following decades of pressure from campaigners, a total of 122 governments signed the Ottawa convention, officially titled 'The Convention on the Prohibition of the Use, Stockpiling, Production and Transfer of Anti-Personnel Mines and on their Destruction' (often referred to as the 'Mine Ban Treaty').

It is the most comprehensive international treaty of its kind, and became law quicker than any other treaty of its kind in history (after less than one year).

But despite worldwide support, and condemnation of the use, sale and stockpiling of anti-personnel land-mines, a total of 37 countries still refuse to sign, including China, Egypt, Finland, India, Israel, Pakistan, Russia and the US.[12] The US refusal has a devastating political influence, giving credence to other countries' refusals. Campaigners continue to demand that these countries drop their opposition to the treaty, and to expand it to cover anti-tank mines and other 'area denial weapons' – a euphemism meaning they blow you up if you stray where you 'should not' – such as cluster munitions and unexploded ordnance.

The treaty has, however, still been a success. As the *Landmine Monitor Report 2008* says, 'use of anti-personnel landmines, especially by governments, has become a rare phenomenon'. It cites Burma and Russia as current users, with allegations (not verified) also made against Sri Lanka. Use by non-state armed groups has occurred recently in at least nine countries: Afghanistan, Burma, Colombia, Ecuador, Iraq, Peru, India, Pakistan and Sri Lanka. The global stockpile of landmines has decreased from over 260 million in the mid-1990s to about 176 million today. 144 of the 156 countries that have signed the Mine Ban Treaty say they do not have anti-personnel mines.

The *Landmine Monitor Report 2008* says: 'For the past decade, global trade in anti-personnel mines has consisted solely of a low-level of illicit and unacknowl-edged transfers'. Many governments (for example, Cuba, China, India, Iran, Pakistan, Russia, Singapore, South Korea, the US and Vietnam) either have anti-personnel mine export moratoria or claim (with varying degrees of plausibility) that they do not export landmines. However, Cuba, the US, Russia, Iran, Nepal, Burma, China, India, North Korea, South Korea, Pakistan, Singapore and Vietnam are still classified as producers of the weapons by the International Campaign to Ban Landmines.

Given that this is a book on the arms trade, it could be argued that the issue should stop there – the trade in anti-personnel landmines no longer exists, and the manufacture is nominal. Unfortunately, the step is not so easily taken.

The Mine Ban Treaty covers only certain types of anti-personnel landmines, leaving vast loopholes where 'area denial weapons', including anti-tank weapons, remain available and traded.

The weapon that has had the highest profile, and where international action has focused, has been the cluster bomb. Usually dropped from a plane, it explodes just above the ground, scattering hundreds of miniature 'bomblets' over a wide area. Many of these bomblets fail to explode, remaining in the ground, just like anti-personnel landmines, until disturbed. Like landmines, unexploded ordnance poses a serious threat to lives and livelihoods.

Cluster bombs were first used by the USSR and Nazi Germany during the Second World War. Beginning with the Vietnam War, cluster bombs have been used regularly in wars across the world in the last 40 years. These have sometimes involved considerable quantities of bomblets or 'submunitions'. In the Gulf War in 1991, an estimated 50 million submunitions were fired, and in the invasion of Iraq in 2003, around 2 million were used. In the 2006 invasion of the Lebanon, up to 4 million submunitions were used by the Israeli Defense Forces.[13]

Landmine Action, while acknowledging the difficulties in documenting the full humanitarian impact of the use of cluster munitions, has argued that their use 'has resulted in a consistent pattern of unnecessary civilian harm'.[14] It cites many examples in its report *Failure to Protect*. In Laos, 11,000 deaths and injuries were caused by unexploded ordnance used in the late 1960s and early 1970s, and it is estimated that around half of these were caused by cluster bombs (dropped by the US). Human Rights Watch noted that by February 2003, 1,600 people had been killed and 2,500 injured in Iraq and Kuwait because of cluster munitions used in the Gulf War of 1991. In the year after the bombing of Kosovo in 1999, the Red Cross reported that cluster bombs were responsible for 82 per cent of accidents involving unexploded ordnance. The Red Cross records that at least 462 Afghans were killed and injured by cluster munitions from 1998 to June 2006.

In February 2007, the Norwegian Government launched the 'Oslo Process', whereby 46 states agreed to create a treaty to prohibit the use, production, export or stockpiling of cluster munitions. In December 2008, 94 governments signed the Convention on Cluster Munitions, which will enter into force once 30 countries have ratified it.

The trade in torture

Torture is prohibited in all circumstances by international law. Torture and inhuman treatment, ill-treatment and degrading practices are the trademarks of repressive states – many of which are supplied with their torture weapons, or political support, by countries which also sell them arms.

Companies and individuals all over the world are involved in supplying devices and expertise, even training, in torture. In some terrible cases, equipment specifically designed for torture is supplied. In others, devices and material that can easily be used for torture are supplied, without hesitation, to police and security forces well known for their techniques in inflicting pain and degrading treatment using whatever tools they can obtain.

Torture equipment and devices such as police batons and handcuffs that can easily be used for torture are shipped under the auspices of arms and are regarded as legitimate goods for sale and purchase by many governments. There are also huge black and 'gray' markets in torture equipment – an illegal market in specially designed weapons, as well as networks of brokers, shippers and fixers ready to exploit loopholes and try legal boundaries in order to profit from equipment sales.

The sale of torture equipment is on occasion still undertaken illegally in Britain.[15] Mark Thomas went in 2007 to IFSEC, a security exhibition held in Birmingham and was offered electro-shock weapons by one exhibitor. Electro-shock weapons are the ultimate weapon of choice for the torturer, who will cover the head or eyes of a victim and administer volts to the most sensitive parts of the body, including the mouth, buttocks and genitals, inflicting maximum pain without leaving permanent marks.

According to Thomas, a Mr Xia, who staffed the stall on behalf of Echo Industrial Company Limited, a Chinese company, 'offered to show me the stun weapons and discharged them in the fair. Electro-shock weapons make a distinct and loud noise. Anyone walking past would easily have seen the blue electrical flashes'. Thomas told a Committee of British MPs that Mr Xia offered to sell him the weapons.

The event organizers, CMP Information Limited, took prompt action, and Mr Xia, who claimed he did not realize what he was doing was illegal under English law, was arrested, given a suspended jail sentence, and subsequently deported.

Handcuffs, leg cuffs, shackles and restraint belts are used all over the world to inflict pain, suffering and degradation on prisoners. Of course, it can be argued that some mechanical equipment, like handcuffs, does have legitimate uses – but in the hands of human rights abusers they can be used directly or indirectly to cause pain. Other devices, like restraint chairs and the rack, have little use except for torture.

Take the case of Sandy Mitchell, a British citizen and former anaesthetic technician at the Saudi Security Forces Hospital in Riyadh.[16] Saudi Arabia is one of Britain's closest allies, yet claimed without any evidence that Mitchell had carried out a terrorist bombing in Riyadh in November 2000. Along with Belgian Raf Schyvens and Briton Bill Sampson, also falsely accused, Mitchell was taken to Mabatha Interrogation Centre south of Riyadh (known as the 'Confession Factory'), forced under torture to confess to the bombings and held for three years without trial.

Mitchell was shackled and severely tortured by the Saudis, and on release was diagnosed as suffering post-traumatic stress disorder and other long-term effects. The shackles were made in Britain, and exported to Saudi Arabia under an export license granted in March 1994. A British Government commitment made in 1997 to ban the export of shackles and other restraint equipment meant the license was revoked, but nothing can be done to prevent people being tortured using equipment made in Britain and exported a decade ago.

Mark Thomas's excellent book *As Used On The Famous Nelson Mandela* documented how even the British Government's commitment to preventing British companies manufacturing, selling or buying torture equipment could be circumvented.[17] A school Amnesty International group in Oxfordshire set up a company, Williams Defence, and were legally able to buy and import into Britain, thumb cuffs, wall cuffs[18] and a 'sting stick' (effectively, as Thomas describes, a 'mass produced version of a club with nails in it'). The reason this was possible is that the British Government regulates torture equipment by listing specific items, rather than having a catch-all clause banning the trade in equipment which could be used for torture.

Exploiting the loopholes: the problem of brokering

Arms brokers are perhaps the most shadowy characters involved in the international arms trade. Operating usually on the very boundaries of legality, if the price is right, they arrange to supply weapons, usually small arms, to the most conflict-prone regions in the world. Brokers are the ones who spend their time on the telephone, organizing shipments from afar, often without having any direct contact with arms themselves. Traffickers are the people who actually shift the arms – transporting, or organizing the transport – but they are of course 'dealing' at the same time as they buy then sell on.

Operating through an intricate network of intermediaries, shipping agents, transporters, corrupt officials and secret contacts, brokers source the second-hand small arms, usually from stockpiles in central and eastern Europe, and supply them to warring factions in Africa, Asia and Latin America. They might never see the arms themselves, and often work in such a way that a route from the arms can never be traced to them. Profits are posted in offshore accounts, front companies are set up and aliases assumed.

But a lack of international co-operation, political will and an ignorance of the extent of the problem means that arms brokers can exploit loopholes in domestic legislation to go about their business with impunity. This is graphically illustrated in *As Used On The Famous Nelson Mandela*, where after-school clubs in Oxfordshire and Ireland successfully start up arms brokering businesses.[19]

In many countries, the traffic of arms only needs permission from the authorities if arms are actually to come in or go out of the country. Arms traffickers

What is an arms broker?

Arms brokers, arms dealers and trafficking agents can be characterized as follows:

• entrepreneurs with military and security backgrounds and contacts;

• motivated by economic gain, not political considerations;

• use loopholes and weak regulations between national legal systems to conduct 'legal' but often unethical business via third countries;

• use transport agents and techniques to conduct clandestine deliveries to clandestine destinations;

• use complex international banking transactions and company formations in many countries, including in tax havens;

• locate sources of cheap, easily transportable arms for desperate customers in areas of violent conflict willing to pay high prices;

• rely on personal contacts and networks, not corporate identities;

• thrive on corrupt officials and weak law enforcement;

• sometimes fake documentation and use bribes, which can lead to involvement in organized crime.

The Arms Fixers – Controlling the Brokers and Shipping Agents, Brian Wood and Johan Palema. A joint report by British American Security Information Council (BASIC), Norwegian Initiative on Small Arms Transfers (NISAT), and International Peace Research Institute, Oslo (PRIO), Nov 1999.

can be resident in one state and arrange an arms shipment between two foreign countries without any fear of punishment. In other cases, where laws are slightly tighter, arms brokers need only step into a country with weaker regulations to make their phone calls, have their meetings and arrange the shipments.

It has been well documented that arms supplied via brokers have gone to some of the world's most brutal conflicts and repressive regimes. The perpetrators of the Rwandan genocide in 1994 were armed by brokers. Brokers also played a role in arming the Angolan rebel movement UNITA, as well as the rebels in Sierra Leone (the Revolutionary United Front). As Amnesty notes, brokering 'was an important additional factor fueling conflicts in Africa and elsewhere'.[20]

In recent years, increasing attention has been

focused on the problem of arms brokering.[21] However, by mid-2005 less than 40 out of 191 UN Member States had specific regulations covering brokering, and most of these were European countries (two-thirds of EU countries had regulations by mid-2005).

The legislation generally seen as the strongest, in the US, was passed in 1996. It requires that a US citizen wherever they reside, or anyone within US territory, must register and seek permission to be involved in an arms transaction. However, it has been criticized by Amnesty for not requiring those involved in the deals but who are not brokers (for example financiers, freight carriers) to register.

The EU, meanwhile, has developed a Common Position on arms brokering (see chapter 9). The Wassenaar Agreement in 2003 agreed a set of common 'elements for effective legislation on arms brokering'. In Britain an arms dealer was jailed in November 2007 after pleading guilty to brokering the sale of 130 machine guns to Kuwait from Iran. The legislation used to convict him was a new law on brokering which came into force in 2004.[22]

Outside Europe there have been regional initiatives in the Americas and Africa, but not Asia and the Middle East. The Organization of American States in 2003 agreed a 'model regulation' for the control of firearms and ammunition, which included provisions on brokering. A lack of political will among American governments means it has not been widely adopted.

In Africa, the Nairobi Protocol, adopted in 2004 by governments in east Africa, the Great Lakes region and the Horn of Africa, required some controls of arms brokering. However, most of these governments have yet to pass laws to comply with the Protocol.

At UN level, progress to control brokering has been slow – in Amnesty's view mainly due to a lack of political will. However, the UN Firearms Protocol, which was negotiated in 2001 and entered into force in

2005, set out some legal obligations for governments to control the brokering of firearms and ammunition. The scope of this is narrow, as it only relates to some types of small arms, so the UN General Assembly has asked for consideration of controls on other types of weapons. Two UN Groups of Governmental Experts have been convened to this end. The latest one issued a report in 2007 with recommendations focusing on national implementation of adequate laws, information sharing between governments, international assistance and capacity building, and effective reporting. The UN Programme of Action on small arms (see chapter 9) has also agreed to develop laws and practises relating to the brokering of small arms.

1 Report of the Panel of Governmental Experts on Small Arms, UN document A/52/298, 27 Aug 1997. **2** The latest statistics produced by the project can be found at www.smallarmssurvey.org/files/sas/home/FAQ.html **3** Oxfam, *Ammunition: the fuel of conflict*, Jun 2006. **4** See footnote 3. **5** See footnote 3. **6** Much of the information in this section is taken from Oxfam, *Ammunition: the fuel of conflict*, Jun 2006. **7** Government Accountability Office, *Stabilising Iraq: DOD Cannot Ensure that US-Funded Equipment Has Reached Iraqi Security Forces*, Jul 2007. **8** *Good conduct? Ten years of the EU Code of Conduct on Arms Exports*, Saferworld et al, Jun 2008. **9** Amnesty International, *Blood at the Crossroads: Making the case for a global Arms Trade Treaty*, ACT 30/011/2008. **10** See www.icbl.org/problem/solution/ban_arguments. **11** www.landmineaction.org/issues/issue.asp?PLID=1010 **12** Landmine Monitor Report 2008, International Campaign to Ban Landmines, 2008. **13** Cluster Munitions Information Chart, Human Rights Watch, Nov 2008. **14** *Failure to protect: A case for the prohibition of cluster munitions*, Landmine Action, Aug 2006. **15** The information below is taken from Defence, Foreign Affairs, International Development and Trade and Industry Committees, Strategic Export Controls: 2007 Review, House of Commons, 23 July 2007, HC117. **16** The information below is taken from Mark Hollingsworth and Sandy Mitchell, *Saudi Babylon: Torture, Corruption and Cover-Up Inside the House of Saud*, Mainstream Publishing, 2006. **17** Mark Thomas, *As Used On The Famous Nelson Mandela*, Ebury Press, 2006. **18** This was legal until July 2006. **19** See footnote 17, chapter 12. **20** Amnesty International, *Dead on Time – arms transportation, brokering and the threat to human rights*, ACT 30/008/2006. **21** Much of the information below is taken from Amnesty International, *Dead on Time – arms transportation, brokering and the threat to human rights*, ACT 30/008/2006, chapters 5 and 9. **22** 'Arms dealer jailed for 4 years', BERR Press Release, 26 Nov 2007.

9 Ending the misery: what are the alternatives?

The United Nations and small arms... The EU Code and Common Position... Other arms control initiatives... The Arms Trade Treaty... Defense diversification... Campaigning.

MANY WOULD BE forgiven for feeling hopeless about the arms trade. The picture painted here is one of an uncontrollable, cash-eating monolith beyond the reach of individual nation states, causing havoc and destruction wherever it visits with no regard for human lives, decency, accountability or even the laws of the countries in which it operates.

Certainly the outlook is bleak. Next to prostitution, the arms business is perhaps the world's oldest and most ingrained profession. But ever since humans first traded weapons, there has been a body of determined, informed and passionate people campaigning for it to be monitored, controlled, curbed – and ultimately, for some – to be abolished.

A combination of research campaigning, monitoring legislation and government policy, letter-writing, public protest and direct action has slowly begun to bring changes. One of the problems campaigners face is that they often do not know how influential their actions are.

Campaigners cannot claim all the credit for the steps that have been taken locally and internationally. Sheer economic pressure and national security concerns have had their own role to play. But campaigners can at least take credit for much of the arms control legislation which has been introduced, and can continue the campaign for it to be tightened up, clarified, extended and renewed.

No-one should be under any illusion that total

abolition of the arms trade, or even comprehensive reduction, could happen overnight – or even over a decade. Economic reality and international security make this no more than a pipedream.

However, what has already been achieved, as outlined below, can be built upon gradually by further well-informed, forceful and passionate campaigning. Every small victory brings a more just and secure world a little bit closer.

UN Programme of Action on Small Arms and Light Weapons

In July 2001, an unprecedented event took place in New York. For the first time, representatives from 189 different nations came together under the auspices of the UN to draw up a Programme for Action for tackling the problem of small arms, albeit only from an 'illegal/black market' emphasis.

Under the Programme, countries commit themselves to do various things, including making the illicit possession or production of guns a criminal offense, destroying surplus weapons, disarming ex-combatants, taking various steps to improve the ability to track weapons and better enforcing arms embargoes. It has, though, significant weaknesses, including no plans on regulating small arms already among the civilian population nor any way of dealing with the problem of guns being transferred to private ownership.[1]

To discuss the implementation of the Programme there are Biennial Meetings of States, the last one occurring in 2008. There was also a conference to review progress in 2006. The 2008 Biennial Meeting discussed reducing illicit arms brokering, improving the management of small arms stocks, and improving international co-operation.

The EU Code of Conduct

On 11 June 1998, the foreign ministers of the then

15 EU member states adopted the European Code of Conduct on Arms Exports. It aimed to set 'high common standards... for the management of, and restraint in, conventional arms transfers by all EU Member States'. It was a politically binding agreement, under which member states agreed to abide by certain criteria when granting arms exports.

Amongst other provisions under the EU Code, member states agreed several criteria against which applications for arms export licenses have to be assessed. The EU agreed:

• To assess the recipient country's attitude towards human rights;

• Not to issue an export license if there is a clear risk the weapons might be used for internal repression by the recipient country, or end user;

• Not to issue an export license if the export would provoke or prolong armed conflicts or aggravate existing tensions, or if the weapons would be used aggressively against another country;

• To assess whether the proposed export would seriously hamper the sustainable development of the recipient country;

• To assess the capability of the recipient country to exert controls on the re-export of the weapons to elsewhere, especially to terrorist organizations.

The Code was the product of decades of campaigning by NGOs and concerned politicians. The British Government, which held the EU presidency at the time, to its credit avidly pushed for adoption of the Code.

Initially, the EU Code fell well short of what campaigners had been hoping for. But, over the last 10 years, significant improvements have taken place:

• A Common Military List of equipment to which the code applied has been drawn up;

• A Common Position on arms brokering has been developed;

Ending the misery: what are the alternatives?

• A regulation concerning the export of equipment for use in torture or capital punishment has been adopted;

• A Users' Guide has been developed and updated;

• Transparency has improved greatly. Countries now report figures to the EU for inclusion in an annual EU report on arms exports. Most EU states now also publish annual reports on arms exports, usually containing additional information.[2]

In 2003, the EU states reviewed the Code and decided to make it a 'Common Position'. Whereas the Code was a political document and not legally binding, a Common Position means all EU States have to ensure their national legislation is compliant with it, and some say it raises the possibility of challenging export licensing decisions in a court of law. The review was completed in 2005 but was only adopted in December 2008, because of a long period of opposition from France.

The Common Position is essentially the same as the EU Code but contains further small improvements. The criteria against which export license applications have to be assessed now apply also to licensed production, arms brokering, and transit licenses. EU States must deny licenses if the equipment to be exported might be used in serious violations of international humanitarian law. All EU States now have to produce their own annual reports on arms exports, as does the EU itself.

The Common Position does not provide a framework for a system of controlling where the armaments end up once they have been sold. There is no provision for verification. This is a glaring omission, since verification, follow-up monitoring and inspection should surely be an integral part of any arms control agreement.

There are many other problems with the Common Position, as there were with the EU Code, including transparency and scrutiny issues. In practice, the EU Code was not very effective, or at least was very liberally interpreted. NGOs such as CAAT and Saferworld have consistently complained about decisions made by the British Government which appeared to go against the Code. The British Government has, since 1998, exported millions of dollars' worth of arms to countries, including human rights abusing countries such as Turkey, Saudi Arabia and China; to developing countries, including Tanzania, South Africa and Kenya; and to countries involved in violent conflicts, including Sri Lanka and Israel. The exports of other Code signatories follow a similar pattern.

Key steps some EU NGOs are calling for to improve the Common Position are: tightening guidance to make it more difficult for governments to adopt a liberal interpretation, introducing standard re-export controls, more extra-territorial controls on arms brokering, and standardized reporting practices.

Other attempts to curb the trade

There are a number of other international initiatives that have been undertaken to curtail certain elements of the arms trade.

The Wassenaar Arrangement – This grew out of Cold War agreements (known as COCOM) to prevent the transfer of sensitive Western technology to Communist East European countries. It now consists of 40 countries, including Russia, the US, many European states, as well as Australia and New Zealand/Aotearoa.

Wassenaar aims to prevent 'destabilizing accumulations' of conventional weapons by contributing 'to regional and international security and stability, by promoting transparency and greater responsibility in transfers of conventional arms and dual-use goods and technologies'.

It set up a system of guidelines for export and

information exchange between participants.[3] It lays out assessment criteria which may be applied to decide whether to export military equipment, including an assessment of the motivation of the buyer, regional stability, economic standing, human rights situation and the likelihood of destabilizing situations.

Like the EU Common Position, Wassenaar requires member states to notify each other when they refuse arms exports according to the criteria, but there is no obligation on other states to refuse similar exports. The whole denial regime is kept confidential.

The UN Register of Conventional Arms – Launched in 1992, the Register was set up as an early warning system for identifying potentially destabilizing arms escalation, and to allow the international community to use diplomatic means to reduce regional tension and prevent conflict.

Member states are requested, but not required, to submit records each year of the arms they have imported and exported, and are invited to supply information about their domestic military holdings. Since 2003, member states have been able to submit information on the import and export of small arms and light weapons. The number of governments doing so is steadily increasing

The main problem with the Register is that it does not require disclosure, and relies on the most transparent states to encourage others to follow their example. Another problem is that information is only supplied to the Register once weapons have been sold, meaning it cannot be used as a way of controlling the transfer of arms before they take place. The Register would be more effective if exports were registered at the time of order rather than of delivery.

Other agreements – There are other international agreements in existence which cover weapons of mass destruction, rather than the trade in conventional weapons with which this book is concerned. These are:

• the Nuclear Suppliers Group which aims to reduce global nuclear proliferation;
• the Global Partnership against the spread of weapons of mass destruction (WMD), which aims to prevent terrorist acquisition of WMD;
• the Australia Group, which aims to ensure export controls that do not enable the development of chemical or biological weapons;
• the Missile Technology Control Regime, which aims to prevent proliferation of missile technology.[4]

The Arms Trade Treaty[5]

In recent years, the main focus of many anti-arms trade campaigners has been the global campaign for an Arms Trade Treaty (ATT). A campaign called Control Arms, which is run by Amnesty, Oxfam and the International Action Network on Small Arms was launched in 2003. The idea of an ATT has been around since the 1990s, and has been initiated by Nobel Peace Laureates, lawyers and NGOs.

The concept of the ATT is quite simple. It would be legally binding, and would bring together states' current international law obligations. All governments that signed up would operate the same high standards, which would make it much more difficult for unscrupulous arms dealers to take advantage of loopholes created by different countries applying different laws and standards. In this way it attempts to address the increasing globalization of the arms industry.

A strong grassroots campaign across the world resulted in December 2006 in the UN General Assembly passing resolution 61/89 by 153 votes to one, with 24 abstentions.[6] The one country voting no was, however, the world's largest arms supplier – the US. Other important arms producing countries abstained – such as China, India, Israel and Russia.

The Resolution required the UN Secretary-General to ask governments for their views on what an ATT should include and 99 governments responded. An analysis by Amnesty showed: 'An ATT needs to be universally fair and objective, should reflect the existing obligations and commitments of States and must address the realities of globalizing markets and international assistance programs in conventional arms.' Most states agreed there should be common standards for the trade in conventional arms, and that respect for international humanitarian law should be one of the criteria used in decisions on arms exports.

In 2007, Amnesty and other leading NGOs published a set of 'global principles for arms transfers', which included 'obligations based on relevant international law treaties and international customary law, principles recognized by the UN, including international human rights law and [international humanitarian law], and principles of state responsibility'. Currently the Control Arms campaign has set out five 'golden rules' they want an ATT to follow. These are that states will not export arms where they will:
• be used or are likely to be used for gross violations of international human rights law or serious violations of international humanitarian law;
• have an impact that would clearly undermine sustainable development or involve corrupt practices;
• provoke or exacerbate armed conflict in violation of their obligations under the UN Charter and existing treaties;
• contribute to an existing pattern of violent crime;
• risk being diverted for one of the above outcomes or for acts of terrorism.

As well as consulting governments, the UN General Assembly resolution required the UN Secretary-General to set up a UN Group of Governmental Experts (GGE), to study the 'feasibility, scope and parameters' of an ATT. This group reported in August 2008. The group reported that because the issues were very complex, further work should be carried out, but that in the mean time governments should ensure their own export controls were of the highest standard.[7]

Following this, a UN General Assembly Committee decided to establish a Working Group to consider the elements in the GGE report where consensus could be achieved. These areas would then be included in a report to be presented to the UN in late 2009, and which would eventually be included in an ATT. At this point 147 states voted in favor, with only the US and Zimbabwe against.

This is undoubtedly highly impressive progress, yet there are still barriers to success, chief among which is the skepticism of leading arms exporters such as the US, China and Russia. Other barriers include the difficulty of enforcing the Treaty and the potential that governments may interpret the ATT so liberally as to continue 'business as usual'.

The challenge of defense diversification

Pushing for diversification into non-defense activities is one of the strongest tools for campaigners to wield in their arguments for the reform of the arms business. Campaigners are often thrown by the challenge: 'Well, what would we produce instead?'

The best response is that arms manufacturers and related industries should pursue research, skill and expertise in creating equipment that does some kind of social good, or further modernizes society, rather than destroying it. This response also addresses peripheral challenges about job losses and economics.

Diversification implies changing governmental emphasis on arms production and sales into researching, manufacture and sale of non-military goods. It also implies diversification at a company level, a process where weapons producers invest money in creating civil goods, at the expense of their military interests, so that they gradually become non-military manufacturers.

Globally, defense diversification is an idea that is unlikely to have its day in the near future. As an example, the British Government set up a Defence Diversification Agency (DDA) in 1999 'to encourage the civil exploitation of defense technology; help inform industry about MoD's future equipment needs; and facilitate the spin-in of civil technology to defense'.[8] The agency had a mere 35 staff when it closed, and because its remit included brokering technology exchanges from the civil sector to improve military capability, it hardly represented a move towards manufacture of civil products instead of military equipment.

The British Government, via the creation of QinetiQ (in July 2001) and Ploughshare Innovation Ltd (from the Defence Science and Technology Laboratory in 2005), did try to spread military technology into the civilian sector. But it also encouraged civilian companies to get involved in competing for military contracts. As the British Government felt it had brought civil and military technology together, it decided to close the DDA in 2007.

But change in the future is possible. Dr Steven Schofield has convincingly argued the case for 'a fundamental shift from military R&D and procurement to a program of investment in civil technologies for major objectives like renewable energy and reduced carbon emissions in the face of a global environmental crisis... The potential exists for a massive expansion of wave and wind power to satisfy up to 50 per cent of the UK's energy needs by 2030, while forming the basis for a major industry employing tens of thousands of workers to satisfy domestic demand and export markets'.[9] This policy would see skilled workers contributing to projects that would help nullify one of the main drivers of future conflict – climate change – while making it more difficult for British governments to participate in disastrous US military adventures abroad or facilitate arms sales to tyrants across the globe.

As Dr Schofield has pointed out, a radical and far-reaching program is needed. Moderate reforms that, for example, suggest canceling Britain's Trident nuclear submarines in favor of spending on conventional forces, or merely denying equipment to governments with poor human rights records, would leave the essentials of the military-industrial base unchanged. As Dr Schofield says: 'If domestic procurement remains at high levels then there will be a strong supply-side dynamic to continue as a leading arms exporter.' Radical and far-reaching action against the arms trade needs to go hand in hand with a 'radical program of disarmament and common security'.[10]

Keep agitating/join a campaign

Anti-arms trade campaigns have their own policies and priorities according to the national situation. Those with a specific interest should refer to the section at the end of this book to find their local anti-arms trade organization.

The Campaign Against Arms Trade in Britain, for example, had three campaign priorities in 2009:
• End all government political and financial support for arms exports;
• End exports to oppressive regimes, countries involved in armed conflict or in regions of tension and countries whose social welfare is threatened by military spending; and
• Promote policies to fully orientate the British economy towards civil production.

A broader view of campaigning

The campaign against arms trading cannot, and should not, be considered in isolation from other concerns of social justice, except perhaps for the sake of convenience. In almost every area of global injustice, the arms trade plays its deadly role. In earlier chapters it was revealed how the trade exacerbates conflict, promotes human rights abuses and worsens poverty in developing countries.

This *No-Nonsense Guide*, I hope, has illustrated how intimately connected the arms business is to a globally unjust, unequal and exploitative system. Curbing or even abolishing the international arms trade is just a small but vital part of working to make our world a more just, equal, healthy and safe place to live for everyone. Anti-arms trade activists can exploit the connections between the weapons industry and global injustice to mount even more effective campaigns.

1 See www.iansa.org/un/programme-of-action.htm **2** Much of the information in this section is taken from *Good conduct? Ten years of the EU Code of Conduct on Arms Exports* (Saferworld et al, June 2008). **3** See www.wassenaar.org/guidelines/docs/Glines_and_Proced,_including_the_IE.pdf **4** Brief information on these can be found in *United Kingdom Strategic Export Controls: Annual Report 2007*, Stationery Office, Jul 2008. **5** Much of the information in this section is taken from *Blood at the Crossroads: Making the case for a global Arms Trade Treaty*, ACT 30/011/2008, chapter 1. **6** http://tinyurl.com/ctbcfj. **7** *Report of the Group of Governmental Experts to examine the feasibility, scope and draft parameters for a comprehensive, legally binding instrument establishing common international standards for the import, export and transfer of conventional arms*, UN document A/63/334, 26 Aug 2008. **8** Much of the information about the DDA is taken from Lord Drayson's statement to the House of Lords on 28 Mar 2007. See Hansard column WS158. **9** Steven Schofield, *Oceans of Work: Arms Conversion Revisited*, British American Security Information Council, Jan 2007. **10** Steven Schofield, *Making Arms, Wasting Skills*, Campaign Against Arms Trade, Apr 2008.

Contacts and resources

List compiled with the help of the Housmans World Peace Database – contact worldpeace@gn.apc.org

INTERNATIONAL
European Network Against Arms Trade (ENAAT)
Umbrella group for European anti-arms trade and peace organizations.
tel: + 31 20 616 46 84
email: info@stopwapenhandel.org
web: www.enaat.org

Amnesty International
Worldwide campaigning human rights movement.
tel: +44 20 7413 5500
web: www.amnesty.org

Stockholm International Peace Research Institute (SIPRI)
Conducts research on questions of conflict and peace.
tel: +46 8 655 97 00
web: www.sipri.org

British American Security Information Council (BASIC)
Independent research organization that analyzes government defense policies.
US tel: +1 202 546 8055
US email: basicus@basicint.org
UK tel: +44 20 7324 4680
UK email: basicuk@basicint.org
web: www.basicint.org

International Campaign to Ban Landmines
tel: +41 22 920 03 25
email: icbl@icbl.org
web: www.icbl.org

International Action Network on Small Arms (IANSA)
An international network of 800 civil society organizations working in 120 countries to stop the proliferation and misuse of small arms and light weapons (SALW).
tel: +44 207 065 0870
email: contact@iansa.org
web: www.iansa.org

NATIONAL
Australia
Australian Anti-Bases Campaign Coalition (AABCC)
tel: +61 2 9698 2954
email: aabcc@zipworld.com.au
web: www.anti-bases.org

Britain
Campaign Against Arms Trade (CAAT)
tel: +44 20 7281 0297
email: enquiries@caat.org.uk
web: www.caat.org.uk

Saferworld
Thinktank on more effective app-roaches to preventing armed conflict.
UK tel: +44 20 7324 4646
Africa tel: +254 20 273 3250/6480
email: general@saferworld.org.uk
web: www.saferworld.org.uk

Canada
Coalition to Oppose the Arms Trade (COAT)
tel: +1 613 231 3076
email: overcoat@rogers.com
web: http://coat.ncf.ca

Germany
BUKO - Kampagne "Stoppt den Rüstungsexport"
tel: +49 421 326045
email: stop-arms-trade@t-online.de

Netherlands
Campagne Tegen Wapenhandel
tel: +31 20 6164684
email: info@stopwapenhandel.org
web: www.stoparmstrade.org

New Zealand/Aotearoa
Peace Movement Aotearoa
tel: +64 4 382 8129
email: pma@apc.org.nz
web: www.converge.org.nz/pma

South Africa
Ceasefire
tel: +27 11 403 53 15
email: stopwar@mail.ngo.za
web: www.ceasefire.org.za

Contacts and resources

Spain
Centre d'Estudis per a la Pau JM Delàs
tel: + 34 93 317 61 77
email: delas@justiciaipau.org
web: www.centredelas.org

United States
Federation of American Scientists (Arms Sales Monitoring Project)
tel: +1 202 546 3300 ext. 193
email: mschroeder@fas.org
web: www.fas.org/asmp

Bite the Bullet!
War Profiteering Education and Action Network
email: bitethebullet@warresisters.org
www.bitethebullet.us

BIBLIOGRAPHY
Mark Phythian, *The Politics of British Arms Sales since 1964*, Manchester University Press, 2000.
Mark Thomas, *As Used On The Famous Nelson Mandela*, Ebury Press, 2006.
Small Arms Survey 2008, Cambridge University Press, 2008.
Solomon Hughes, *War on Terror, Inc: Corporate Profiteering from the Politics of Fear*, Verso, 2008.
Andrew Feinstein, *After the Party*, Jonathan Ball, 2007.

Index

Index

Index